THE S.P.A.R.K.S. BLUEPRINT™

to Marketing for Local Trades

James Dewane

Herkimer Publishing

First edition
ISBN 978-1-910815-70-0

A catalogue record for this book is available from the British Library.

Published by Herkimer Publishing, United Kingdom
www.herkimerpublishing.com

Design & Typesetting by Lorenzo Guescini / Mystic Mouse® Design

Illustrations by Liwiljo

Printed in the United Kingdom

Foreword

by Tommy Walsh

I first met James, back in 2009, when filming a series for Discovery called, "Fix your house for Free!" James made it very apparent, that helping tradesmen make the best of their business, was one of his major passions. As a tradesman myself, (I use that term very loosely!) I know all too well, that just because you are an excellent tradesmen, it doesn't necessary follow, that you will be a successful business man.

The S.P.A.R.K.S. Blueprint, is written by someone, who obviously knows their trade, and has experienced the highs and lows, of trying to build a profitable and sustainable business. James has years of experience, and through that experience has developed a ground breaking system, which he shares with you in this book, and he travels the country espousing the virtues of this system, to anyone wishing to listen and learn!

The book's an easy read, and in language that tradesmen should understand. James has broken down marketing into bite-size chunks to avoid the reader being overwhelmed, plus each section can be dipped into, when necessary. "Well done James" for broaching this subject, in the "world of trades" a subject rarely touched upon, yet hugely important if you want your business to do well!

I'm delighted James has decided to share his ideas in print, as I think this book will be a great asset, to all tradesmen, not just electricians.

Regards

Tommy Walsh

TV Personality and "the Don of DIY"
August 2015

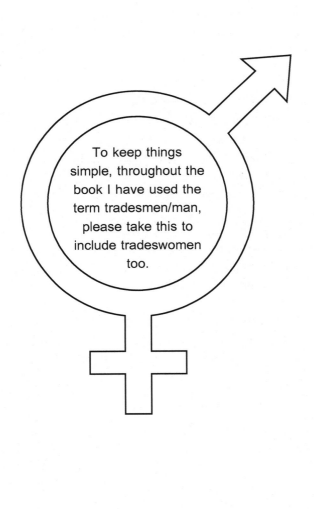

To keep things simple, throughout the book I have used the term tradesmen/man, please take this to include tradeswomen too.

ToolBox tales...

*I attended a webinar hosted by James and as a result of the amount usable information he shared, I decided to sign up to **My Electricians ToolBox™**. I wanted to learn how to develop a strategy for growing my business.*

At the time I joined there was no other electrician in Ireland in the ToolBox and I thought it would be very UK focused; however In a short period of time I was seeing great results in my business and I know it is still only in the early stages. I feel that I now have greater control over my business and confidence in promoting it.

Being a member has been a great help to me as there is knowledge sharing, new ideas, problem solving and, in general, it is great to have like minded 'go to' people when I need some assistance.

Membership will be really useful for people who are great technically, but perhaps are not business and marketing savvy. It is very difficult to find any training, courses, websites etc that could provide you with all of the practical tips and advice that the ToolBox gives .

I would absolutely recommend it.....as long as you are not in my area!

Francis McKevitt,
McKevitt Electrical
www.mckevittelectrical.com

ToolBox tales...

As you have helped me so much, I wanted to drop you an email about my success. I was doing a lot of sub contracting within factory's and the majority of it was getting me down, but after several months of using your ideas (and my work ethic), I managed to drop all my sub contracting and now all work is my own.

The ToolBox itself is fantastic idea, it is full of brilliant content that's always fresh and up to date. It's well worth the money - even if I only use one bit of advice a month, then it's worth it.

I am now in 5 magazines across two counties, and I would say 80% of my work comes from that, My yell.com reviews are now more than any electrician in Worcester: this has generated more work and 'blown a lot of my competition away' - my customers words not mine.

I must thank you again James for the chance to control what I do in my working life. Even though it's early day's, without your advice I don't think I would be in this position. Again you have to put the work in to make it work, so I am also proud of the way I do it, but there is always room for improvement and these little tweaks here and there can make all the difference.

Darren Spencer
Darren Spencer Electrical
www.darrenspencerelectrical.co.uk

Acknowledgements

There are a number of people without whose help I could never have created this book, or any of my training programmes.

Firstly I must thank my wonderful wife who has been so patient when I was stealing family time to sit and work on chapters. As I finish writing this in the summer of 2015 we are just four weeks away from our tenth wedding anniversary, so she has been through thick and thin with me, and without her support I would have thrown the towel in long ago!

I must then thank three people who were instrumental in making me believe and understand that you can achieve anything if you just put your mind to it. Justin Jones and Shai Meirav; I worked closely with these two during a real transformational part of my life and they both left their positive marks. Also, Mick Jessup, without whose support I would quite literally not be where I am today. Mick has supported me in many ways – he has been a rock, a big brother, a father and a friend all rolled into one.

Then there is my old boss Louis Dunne, who intervened and offered me an apprenticeship back in 1983 weeks before I was due to join the Royal Electrical and Mechanical Engineers. My apprenticeship under Louis, and his son Martin, provided me with a real understanding of the trade of an electrician. Louis will understand when I say with affection that he was a hard taskmaster, but a fair boss. I will always be grateful for the trade that Louis gave me.

Thanks to my parents, including my stepdad, who have supported me through the hard times, of which there were many. To survive in any business you need both the moral and financial support of others and my mother and stepdad have been there through thick and thin too. They have been there, not just to pick me up when I fell, but to kick my arse when it needed it – yes, even at 48 years old!

I believe in having mentors and learning from others and as far as my adventure into teaching marketing is concerned there have been three important influences. There's Nick James – he set me on the path I am currently on, Nick saw that I had something to share with other tradesmen, then showed me how to do it. Nigel Botterill is another phenomenal businessman, and as a member of his Entrepreneur's Circle I learned a huge amount as I masterminded with him and eight other great businessmen and women. Then more recently there is Andy Harrington and his Public Speakers University and Professional Speakers Academy, where I spent a further eighteen months learning how to package what I teach and present it. Public speaking doesn't come naturally to me, in fact I don't know many who it does come easily to, but with Andy's teaching and his team's support it has made speaking something that I now enjoy.

The team at Herkimer Publishing – to Lorenzo Guescini, who has been responsible for layout and typesetting; I thank you for producing such a great visual feast. Sharon Lynn has been instrumental in helping to get my words into print. Those who know me will know that writing doesn't come easy to me and my spelling and grammar leave a lot to be desired; Sharon has ensured that my words made sense and she has also provided the occasional nudge towards a deadline when I have been slack. If you are considering writing a book, I suggest you start by talking to the guys at www.HerkimerPublishing.com

My illustrator Liwiljo is responsible for the pictures that pepper this book. Liwiljo has been a pleasure to work with. You can find more of his work at www.liwiljo.carbonmade.com

I can't possibly mention everyone here, so if you have not personally been acknowledged it does not mean I value your help, contribution or assistance less than any other.

Thank You!

James

THE SPARKS

BLUEPRINT to Marketing for Local Trades

Contents

Introduction

The S.P.A.R.K.S. Blueprint™

HAVING WORKED IN the domestic sector of the electrical industry for over twenty five years, I have seen many changes; from types of training, changes in regulations and working practices to advances in materials and components used.

Unfortunately, there is one area that doesn't seem to have changed – the failure rate of people who set up as domestic contractors. Around 80% of tradesmen and women that start up in business will fail within the first couple of years. This isn't because they are not skilled at what they do, they fail because no one has ever shown them how to get and keep good customers.

You may have experienced one or both of the following scenario's when you first set up in business. These are common situations that most tradesmen find themselves in and I have experienced both.

The first scenario is the typical situation where you decide to go it alone. Maybe you reach a point in your work life where lots of family and friends are asking you to do small private jobs for them and you find yourself working weekends and holidays. You seem to have plenty of private work coming in and you think there is now enough for you to take the plunge, so you set up on your own.

However, it's not long before you find that the initial glut of work dries up and you have no idea how to get new customers. You end up doing what everyone else does, you advertise in the local paper, you pay someone to build a website and maybe pay for SEO (Search Engine Optimisation) or even worse you pay for leads and find that it's a never-ending money pit with diminishing returns. Any of this sound familiar?

The second scenario is that you might be lucky enough to be in an area where finding customers isn't a huge issue as long as you can pay the advertising rates. But, you find you are working just as hard trying to get the customer in the first place as you are doing the actual job. So, your days are busy working on the tools and your evenings are taken up trying to fill your diary.

As I mentioned, I have been in both situations so I know what it's like. I know the fear of looking at an empty diary and not knowing where the next job or pay packet is coming from. I know the frustration of handing money over, month after month, for advertising that doesn't work, along with the annoyance of turning up to do a quote from a paid for lead only to find it's not a genuine one, or, that five other electricians have also been out to quote for the job you thought was yours.

After my previous business failed I had a huge 'light bulb' moment (if you'll pardon the pun!). It's one that I think all tradesmen would benefit from before they set out on the path of self-employment or business ownership, and it's this:

It doesn't matter how good a tradesman you are; if you don't have customers you don't have a business!

That's not to say you shouldn't be good at your trade. You should, of course, be the best you can be in order to deliver a great service to your customers, but you need to give equal weight to the marketing of your business and unfortunately no one ever tells you this piece of important information during your apprenticeship or on the job training. I am guessing I'm right when I say that no one ever told you that you would need to be a marketer of what you do and not just a doer of your craft or skill.

It's important, now more than ever before, that you learn how to market your services because we have a greater influx of electricians, domestic installers and all manner of other trades entering our industry at this time, and, as the economy recovers this is going to increase due to the fact that many of those qualified electricians and domestic installers who are currently in employment will begin to feel secure enough to try self-employment. It's possible that you are one of those people who has sat out the recession in the comfort of paid employment and feel with the recovery under way now is the time to get out on your own.

Back when I was an apprentice it was difficult to become an electrician, there were many hoops to jump through to become an apprentice and a full apprenticeship was the only route to becoming an electrician. The town I grew up in had less than a handful of qualified electricians who had a large pool of work to earn their living from. Today there are many routes to becoming an electrician or a domestic installer, there are even ways to become qualified as a tester and inspector without ever qualifying as an installer. Now, it is not my place to judge whether this is right or wrong, but it means that there is a lot of competition out there now all targeting the same customer. Your potential customer!

Learning how to market yourself efficiently and cost effectively will set you head and shoulders above all of the other players out there and ensure that you will get a constant flow of work.

Would you like to get more quality customers?

Would you like to know how to get those quality customers?

Wouldn't it be great to know how to get them easily and consistently?

Wouldn't it be helpful if those customers come back to you time and time again?

Wouldn't it be even better if they also brought with them their family, friends and colleagues?

If you answered 'yes' to any or all of these questions then continue to read this book and discover the **six simple steps** that you need to take in order to ensure that you get your diary filled with good quality customers, that not only come back to you time and again, but they also rave about your work and are consistently recommending you, ensuring that you always have a steady flow of local quality work.

Chapter 1

Drinking, Debt and Determination

O N A DREARY, wet October day in 2007 you and I are aimlessly wandering the streets of Bromley. I am in a complete daze and literally have no idea which way to turn and you have no idea how to help me. I turn to you in utter desperation.

"What do I do now!? Where do I go!?"

You try to reassure me but I continue in my despair.

"My wife and I have got a baby on the way and we've just committed to buying our new home in Kent, and now I don't even have the bus fare home! How did this happen? I've just come out of a meeting with my friend Rob. I've known him for almost three years and I thought he was going to advise me how I get through this situation. He was supposed to help me! Instead I have come away with nothing, literally nothing!"

Rob is a financial adviser who specialises in helping companies who find themselves in trouble and I had just walked out of the office of my friend – who had just become my liquidator. He told me that due to the financial state of my company, I could not legally trade anymore, not for one more second. So, I could no longer trade and I had to tell my staff that I had nothing left and I could not pay them. I was declared insolvent! I would also have to explain to my wife that our plans for a new home were in jeopardy. I felt a complete failure.

This morning I was a businessman, I had a thriving company, and employed nine staff, with three vans and a car on the road plus a nice little shop front office in South London. Now I had nothing; no business. In effect I was unemployed, my vans and car were company property so I couldn't use them nor could I access my company bank accounts.

Even so, I was determined I was not about to become bankrupt. I had lost my business and had no idea how I was going to avoid personal bankruptcy, especially as I had borrowed heavily and just committed to a mortgage on a new house. I owed a lot of money and all I had now was my hand tools!

Friends and family had helped me financially when I was building the business and the bank had trusted me with personal and business loans; any one of them could have pushed the bankruptcy button by forcing a repayment, meaning the new house and car and even the shirt off my back would have been gone and I could easily have been declared bankrupt, but, I managed to convince everyone to have some further faith in me and thankfully they did!

Now I had to dig really deep and start again. I had no money for adverts, no money for marketing or staff. Nothing. All I had was my hand tools, my wife's car and the sheer determination that I was not going to fail again. That was it!

So, how did I get here!?

Let me take you back to the beginning...

I was born and raised in Ireland and grew up in a little place called Tullamore. Like you and many other tradesmen of that era, I did a four year apprenticeship and worked for a small family firm. I didn't realise or appreciate it at the time, but Louis Dunne was the best mentor a young budding electrician could have. He was, I thought, a hard task master, but for all the right reasons and I owe my work ethic to this man. He never believed anything was impossible; to him it was just a matter of discovering how. He was well liked and respected in our local town and I was lucky to have served my apprenticeship with him.

Once I had completed my apprenticeship I decided I would have a 'foreign' holiday as I'd never been out of Ireland. So at eighteen I took myself off to London for a week.

In those days there was no Ryanair or easyJet, yes, you could fly Aer Lingus but back then a ticket would have been about six months wages, so I took a bus that boarded a ferry in Dublin and then after landing in Wales it took us all the way down to London. The final stop was Euston station, where I jumped on the first red London bus and said to myself "wherever it stops that's where I'll get off and have my holiday!" I got on the number 73 and it took me to a place called Stoke Newington. The bus stopped outside a pub, so I ventured in and asked if they knew of a local B&B. The barman told me that they let out some rooms above the bar, so I ended up staying there!

There was often live music in the bar which I thought was great and early into my stay I met a lovely young London girl – my planned one week stay turned into two; two weeks turned into a month and the upshot is I stayed there for six years, even though my mum and other family members back home, weren't best pleased! I got by for a while as I was working in the bar temporarily but I kept thinking to myself "if I'm going to stay then I've got to get a proper job".

For a while I went from job to job, Barman, Store Detective (that could be a chapter on its own), builder's labourer and eventually, being a qualified electrician I found a job with a Kent based company and settled into a career 'house bashing'. The company ran teams (or gangs) of three electricians and we worked on council houses, knocking these things out pretty rapidly. I spent several years with them having been made up to foreman quite early on, which was all very well and good but I thought "Why am I earning all this for someone else? I'm running these teams, I'm doing all the purchasing, I'm controlling the work that's being done. Why do all that for this guy when I could do it all for myself?" I realise now that this is a common affliction for employees in the trades. It's normal to reach the point where you feel "I know enough now to go it alone"... I bet you have experienced that feeling at least once.

So, I eventually gave in my notice, got my own van and set up as Medway Electrical Services. I knew my stuff and I was a good electrician, but I was absolutely clueless about how to actually get any work. Once work from friends and family dried up, I had no idea how to get more. I did all the usual things – got business cards printed, put ads in the paper and even ended up putting an advert in the Yellow Pages that cost me £600. I received just one phone call from that £600 advert and even that offered up no work!

Lots of money went down the proverbial drain and needless to say, the business didn't last more than about six months – so I had to give up my dream. I had borrowed money from my family and my wife's family which put a lot of strain on our relationship, ultimately I ended up divorced and had to fold the business.

I felt a complete failure and hid myself away for a bit. This was a very low point in my life I can tell you; I started drinking, and let's say, I was having more alcohol than is 'normal'. However, I knew I needed to get back into employment somehow, but having had these experiences with being an electrician I did not want to go back into the trade. It was at this time I found a job in the security industry.

Despite all of this, me being me, I worked my way up the ranks in the industry I found myself in – but I was not happy just being a security guard so, I worked hard and sought promotions, first to supervisor, then contract manager. It was at this point I was head hunted by a large security consultancy who were looking to enter the UK market in open access security, I worked on some prestigious projects, consulting on the O2 and London Eye during their construction phase, also setting up security systems for hospitals and universities across the UK and Ireland.

I took the company up on an offer to study and ended up with a degree in Business Management and Marketing from the Open University. I eventually became the Regional Manager and was responsible for operations in the whole of the UK and Ireland. This was a great period in my life with some excellent work colleagues and extensive travel. I would attend meetings in Rome, Israel, Greece and many other beautiful places, or at least what I saw of them passing through seemed nice. You don't actually really get to see much of these places when you're moving from airport to hotel into a meeting room and then back to the airport.

Although I was working really hard during my time in the security industry, I was also playing pretty hard and drinking to excess. In fact, I was, what was known as, a fully functioning alcoholic. I remember a lunch meeting with my boss one day where I had downed a substantial amount of alcohol and he asked "is it normal for you to drink like that at lunch"? For me it was normal and I didn't see an issue with it, after all I didn't feel drunk and could function (I thought), his advice to me was – "If you have a drink like that at lunch you shouldn't really be at work".

My mentality at the time was that if the boss said I shouldn't go back to work after a drink at lunchtime, that I would still have a drink at lunchtime and take the rest of the day off. It never occurred to me that he was suggesting I shouldn't actually be drinking at all at lunchtime! I really don't know how I got away with it.

In a little over four years though we had taken the company from a small entry operation at £8 million turnover to £28 million with around four hundred staff in twelve offices across the UK and Ireland.

Anyway, eventually the company was bought out by a major airline and the management team were given an opportunity to stay on as part of the new management or to take redundancy. My gut was telling me that the new owners would make big changes and that I may not have the autonomy I had previously enjoyed. I had also been thinking about going back to my trade, I figured "now I've got a degree and I know a little more about how to run a business, I'll start again".

I really wanted to go back to working for myself, so I took a refresher course and updated my qualifications in the trade. The redundancy money was spent on two vans, two sets of tools to kit out the vans and I set up a little office in South Norwood where I ultimately employed nine people and had a number of contracts with property developers. There was a pretty sizeable turnover – but there was rarely any profit. Turnover and profit you soon find out are very different. On paper the business looked good and sustainable, but a great turnover is not always a sign of success. More often than not, the lads got paid and I got nothing! I seemed to be running the business just for the sake of running the business.

Then came the time when the two developers we were working with went under in close succession owing me in excess of £40,000. They both went down and defaulted on payments. Now, £40,000 may not sound like a lot to some, but this completely screwed up my cash flow which was always a bit tight anyway due to payment terms. I got to a point where I couldn't pay bills and I was having sleepless nights. I had lots of work in the pipeline and a good team of staff but because my cash flow was screwed so was I... I had a couple of options that I explored without success. One option was to sell the company and clear the debts, which could have worked because the buyer would have had a thriving company up and running and I could have walked away debt free, but the clock was ticking, time was against me and my hand was being forced; so I went to see my friend Rob for some advice...

So here is where you found me on that October day in 2007, in the state I was in after visiting my friend. You see, I had no choice but to appoint 'my friend' the liquidator and hand him the keys to my business.

Here again for the second time, in my mind, I was a failed businessman.

"Where do I turn? What do I do? Do I go home? Do I go to the pub? (By now I had been sober for almost seven years). What do I tell everyone? How do I explain it to my wife? How will things ever be okay again?"

Yes you find me feeling sorry for myself, with just my hand tools and my wife's car left as the only means of transportation, but I had to start again, I had no choice. I had a new home, a family to support and people I didn't want to let down, I didn't have time to wallow or get depressed. I had to get out and earn some money. Sometimes you have to hit rock bottom before you see things for what they really are. I resolved to start again with a determination that I was never going to fail again, especially as everyone I owed money to had faith in me and trusted that I would rebuild a business and pay them back in good time. If they saw this in me, then I couldn't let them down, I would dig deep and deliver.

I reached out to a couple of friends, not for loans, but to find work – one was a hairdresser called Bobby. He owned a salon and needed some electrical work doing. So I went and spent a few days working in his salon doing some odds & sods for him. During the time I was there, people were coming and going all the time, some would ask if I could quote on things for them, others would book me there and then to do small jobs. I realised that while the work at the hairdressers was going on I was picking up a lot of other work – all domestic and without doing any advertising. It got me thinking "what are the best cheap or low cost ways of getting work? How could I go about getting work without having to get involved with builders, agencies, or developers so that I could get my own work? That way the likes of those kind of companies couldn't let me down again."

It became obvious that I should target the domestic market. The nice thing about working in the domestic market is that when you do direct work for homeowners there's no expectation on their part of them paying in 30 days or 60 days. Their thinking is "when I want the job done I'll have the money to pay for the job", so it's payment on completion of work done for you (instead of waiting around for an invoice to be paid) and that is great for cash flow. So I decided I was sticking purely with the domestic market and I would investigate every single way I could to get work cheaply, or at no cost at all, it became a bit of an obsession for me.

My heavily pregnant wife and I had by then moved to Kent and I had to decide if I was going to carry on travelling every day to deal with clients in London (as there is always work and money there), or if I was going to try and build a business locally. I made the decision that if I was starting small and building up again I had to start to find work nearby and so I looked at different methods and ways of how to get work much closer to home – again at little or no cost. At this point friends and family members called me crazy, they told me I should keep the business in London especially as I had some customers from the old business, and finding work in London wasn't difficult.

I had no customers in Kent and had no idea how many other electricians I would be competing against for work. I was now working alone, and I knew if I was to commute every day there was no way I could build the business. If I was just working, driving and doing paperwork I would never be able to earn any real money; so the commute had to go and I would put a stake in the ground and build a local business.

"My challenges became my obsession and my obsession became my passion"… and as a result I studied everything I could about marketing and in particular local marketing. There was nothing out there for tradesmen so I looked at other sectors and figured out how to adapt marketing tactics

and techniques used in those sectors and make them effective for me as an electrician. I attended workshops, went on short courses, weekend seminars, read books and bought audio & video programs. I also studied hypnosis and basic NLP (Neuro Linguistic Programming) and as my business grew I joined mastermind groups and subscribed to newsletters & magazines from marketing experts in the US and the UK. In truth I spent a small fortune learning what works and, more importantly, what doesn't.

Chapter 2

Bacon Sarnies and Luminous Post-its

A FEW YEARS INTO my recovery, the period where I was working my butt off to claw my way back to success, I was involved with BNI (Business Network International). Just in case you are not familiar with them, they run weekly networking breakfasts where you get to meet other local businesses and help one another to get more customers or clients.

These events are held in almost every town worldwide and are a very effective way to get business. All groups will allow you to attend two or three times for free to see if you are a match for the group and vice versa. It's amazing how many tradesmen say that they don't find these meetings work very well for them, but my philosophy is 'it works, if you work it'. I was involved with a very active group who not only shared business leads but also shared experiences, so you learned what was working for others and often were able to test out ideas and plans on people of a similar mind-set. Going to these networking meetings made me realise three things.

These three things would later help me to create the S.P.A.R.K.S. Blueprint™:

- It is possible to find customers for very little or no financial investment
- It is very important to niche your market (be specific)
- It takes very little additional effort to get a new customer to rave about you and bring you repeat business

Now, there was a selection of lads from various other trades attending these groups, and some of us used to meet informally outside of BNI for a further chat about our businesses (these days this would be called a power group or mastermind).

We'd meet in a local builders café every Thursday morning, have a chat and a bit of breakfast and there was always a conversation about what the d***head was doing this week. Meaning me! This came about because I was always up to something quirky, trying to see if it would work to get more business; like putting stickers on coins and using luminous Post-it notes, coupons or setting up joint ventures for example.

One Thursday morning, with the usual smell of coffee and bacon in the air and the sound of the bacon sizzling, some noisy chatter and the background hum of Radio 1 – the door flies open. Scott, all dressed in black, thunders in. He's like a younger version of Father Ted with just a little less hair.

"I'll have me usual please love!" he barks.

Then turning to me, he raises his hands in front and makes a capital "T" with his two index fingers, the international builder sign language for "do you want a cup of Tea"? I motion back with my left hand thumb and index finger formed in the shape of a "C" for Coffee as it saves shouting across the café. Just a few moments later Scott pulls up a chair and sits with the group.

"So what's the d***head talking about this week?" referring to me again. One of the guys brings him up to speed while I continue to explain to the rest of the group about the new vinyl stickers I was now using on one pound coins.

As our informal meeting drew to a close and the guys drift away to their various vans and pick-ups – I notice that a guy who had been sat off to my right was now approaching the table with two cups in hand. I recognised him from being in the café regularly but didn't know him personally. He sidled over to me.

"Coffee" he said, indicating that the second mug was for me. "Can I have a word?"

"Sounds serious" I thought. So I sat back down.

"I need to have a chat....excuse my language, but I'm f**ked!"

"What d'you mean?"

"There are bailiffs coming on Monday to take my van and I don't know what to do! I know you have been through this and just thought you would know what I should do."

I'm thinking "how the hell does he think I can help him?"

In my head, I'm saying "you let it get a bit close if they're coming on Monday – as it is Thursday already!"

After a brief conversation it appears he has a relatively new business and because work was a bit slow he has missed some van payments in favour of paying his mortgage. I'm wondering now what I can do to help this guy. Can I help him get some business quick smart? Hindsight being a wonderful thing, I realise now he might actually have been trying to ask me for a loan!

"How much have you got to come up with?"

"About three grand."

So after a few cups of coffee and a long chat about his business, the type of customers and the work that is best for him I said "Okay – so what we can do is this..." He looks at me blank and bemused! Naively, I'm still not realising he maybe wanted that loan and he clearly had no clue why I was about to show him how to get some business.

I outlined a plan, I told him it wouldn't be easy and between now and Monday there would be a lot of leg work; but if he was prepared to listen and do as I suggested, I believed that we could raise the money to save his van.

My plan centred on having a great offer (great value for the customer), creating a deadline to accept the offer (you'd be crazy not to) and then getting the offer in front of the right people.

There was no time or money to get professional leaflets done so we went back to his house after a visit to Staples for all the supplies and we designed and printed our own; just like I had done a few years previously when I was starting again. Paul's printer only printed on one side, so we waited while one batch dried and then ran them through on the other side creating double sided leaflets – four to every A4 sheet. His wife and daughter got busy with the guillotine. A ream of 500 sheets gave us 2,000 leaflets. All the while Paul is openly saying "This will never work, we're wasting our time."

Regardless, we pressed on and when the leaflets were ready we left his wife and daughter to finish preparing the remainder while went to deliver them through the doors of the affluent homes in the area, despite him still shaking his head saying "This will never work!"

Within an hour of starting to drop these leaflets, Paul started to take calls and bookings came in for quotes to do work. By Saturday he had collected over £5,000 for deposits of work that he would do in the coming weeks. So when the bailiffs came on Monday to collect his van, they collected money instead.

Now, I should point out that Paul was not an electrician, but by applying some of the simple stuff I was able to show him it helped him get back on his feet. Paul has gone from strength to strength and now employs three staff and has an industrial unit that he works out of.

Thursday morning in the café after that I wasn't a joke anymore! More people joined us at the table and it seemed that people were thinking "If James can do it for himself, and, do it for Paul – maybe he can do it for us too!"

Many of the guys suggested that I should do more with this, but no one knew what that meant. There was nowhere to go and teach this stuff, or so I thought. So I continued to entertain in the café and use my BNI ten minute presentation to talk about local marketing but there was always an undercurrent of ... **"James, you should do more with this!"**

I was always looking for fresh low cost ideas for marketing and eventually came to a point where I wanted to try using video, to put videos on my website and create a YouTube channel. As usual I didn't want to depend on someone else to do this for me. I wanted to learn how to do it myself, so I would know if it worked or didn't. Like all my marketing methods, even if I outsource them later to save time, I will still learn what's involved. By doing this I know the value of what I'm paying for and get a feel for whether it's a good fit for my business or not.

Anyway, I searched online for training and courses on how to create videos. At this time other industries were using video to advertise or market their services and lots of amateurs were doing 'how to' style videos on YouTube but not many tradesmen were using this mix for local marketing. However, I had a feeling I could make this work for me. During my search to create affordable online videos I found loads of courses, some really expensive and some not so. I attended workshops in Birmingham and London and then one day while online I came across a guy called Nick James. Nick teaches business and marketing, mainly in the coaching sector, but he was running a workshop on how to market your business through video. From his promotional video it looked like the exact thing I had been searching for.

The workshop was only £95 so I booked my place. It was a great day full of really practical information and towards the end of it Nick invited people to come to the bar afterwards and have a chat. I was impressed by the presentation and what I had learned during the day, even though some of it was contrary to a few of the other courses I had attended, but Nick made making video look so easy to do, so I stayed behind. It is these simple techniques that he taught me that I now teach my students and other tradesmen just like you.

At some point in the evening I got talking with Nick and he expressed some surprise at seeing me at his event. He said "I normally work with trainers and coaches, I have life coaches, NLP practitioners, business coaches but it's unusual to see a tradesman at one of these events." We talked for quite a while about all the different things I had been trying. We examined some of my failures and looked at the successes. I told him the story about Paul and how I have the informal meetings with friends where we discuss some of my tactics.

"Why are you not teaching this? Why aren't you telling other tradesmen how to market their business? Look, if you are telling me there is no one in your industry that does this and there are people failing because they don't know this simple stuff, then you are doing yourself, and them, a big disservice by not sharing what you know!"

He continued "James, I don't pretend to know how life does this, but you have ended up on my course today and sitting here with me this evening for a reason, and I think that reason is so I can tell you that YOU NEED TO BE TEACHING OTHERS!"

A lot of tradesmen who fail in business fail not because they are bad at their trade (often they are excellent tradespeople) they fail simply because they don't know how to market their business. They just don't know how to get the work they need to survive and thrive. I really enjoy trying new things and seeing them work, but I get a much bigger kick out of showing others how to do the things I discovered and then watch them get results too.

"Maybe Nick's right" – my little voice said. "Maybe I should do something with this...Maybe no one else is doing this because it's supposed to be me."

But then you know when the other little voice kicks in and says something like "Who the f**k do you think you are? Who would listen to you anyway? Why would anyone bother? Yeah it's a good idea, but I'm not the person to do it."

So I did nothing... and left it.

I learned how to do the video side of things and I put a selection of videos on my site as planned. I built a YouTube channel and almost instantly started to get results from just a small technique and tactic that I had learned and was using.

Several weeks passed and I was out on the tools one day when my phone rang. It was Nick.

"Hey James did you give any thought to what we talked about?"

I told him I hadn't thought any further on it as my electrical business was doing well and I was focused on that. Like a red rag to a bull he said...

"What is it you're afraid of?"

Me...afraid!?

"You can't be afraid of others knowing what you know, because you know there is more than enough work out there, so it's nothing to do with the competition. You can't be afraid that your tactics and systems don't work, because you are filling your diary and from what you tell me so are some of your friends...So what is it?"

He continued "You know that I help coaches and trainers build their businesses, and I know it's not what you're doing right now but I am excited about what you are doing and really believe you could coach and train others to do the same. I run a mastermind that I believe will help you, we are a group of trainers and coaches from various sectors all helping one another."

I told him I wasn't sure it was for me but he convinced me to meet with him at his home so he could tell me more about it. I went to that meeting and the rest as they say is history; I joined Nick's mastermind group. I learned how to run webinars and started to do them monthly, teaching local marketing tactics to electricians. And, through working with Nick I also wrote a simple e-book which you may even have read 'The Electricians Business Blueprint'. If you have not seen this yet then please visit **www.jdewane.com/gifts**

People were buying the e-book and attending my webinars! I realised there was a real need for what I was doing, yes there were marketing 'Gurus' out there selling all sorts of generic packages and there were people who never spent a day in a real business proclaiming that they could teach you how to find customers. What I was doing was 'real world' stuff; I was teaching what I was using and what was working for me in real life situations, not some broad theory that was applied to every 'Entrepreneur'.

What was really interesting was that weeks and months after the e-books went out I was receiving emails from electricians using them, saying things like:

"I've started to use your stuff and I'm getting results!"

"I've started using leaflets your way, and they are working! I had tried them before and couldn't make them work."

"I've changed my website and I've done what you suggested and people are responding."

"I never liked networking and never really saw the point but now I enjoy it and get work from it."

I was getting some really great feedback and people started asking where they could learn more.

I left it for a while before I did anything else, and then came an opportunity to attend a seminar and go and see a guy called Andy Harrington. Andy teaches public speaking, but not the old school way, he teaches you how to package your knowledge into workshops and training courses and shows you how to deliver what you know so that others can benefit. Nick had spoken very highly of Andy, so I went to see what he had to share and how I could put it to use.

I joined Andy's program and attended many meetings, learning how to package and deliver training. I studied public speaking & coaching and also became a member of the Association of Professional Coaches, Trainers & Consultants (APCTC). It was at this stage in the journey that I built what is now a very successful Membership Program:

My Electricians ToolBox™
www.jdewane.com/bookoffer

My Electricians ToolBox™ is the only resource like it in the UK. It is where I house all of my training on marketing for tradesmen. It has Tools, Software, Training, Downloads and Help Sheets... everything a tradesman could need to market their business locally. Today we have members from not only the UK and Ireland but also as far away as Canada, the US and even Australia; all using and benefiting from this valuable resource.

With Andy's help I also put together the program of practical workshops that I now run across the UK and Ireland. You can get details about these on **www.jdewane.com/live**

Then he suggested I should write a book!

No surprise that I had the same old doubts pop up, but they were short lived and I figured why not?! So, in the following chapters you will discover my simple six step system to marketing a Local Service Based Business...**The S.P.A.R.K.S. Blueprint™** to Marketing for Local Trades.

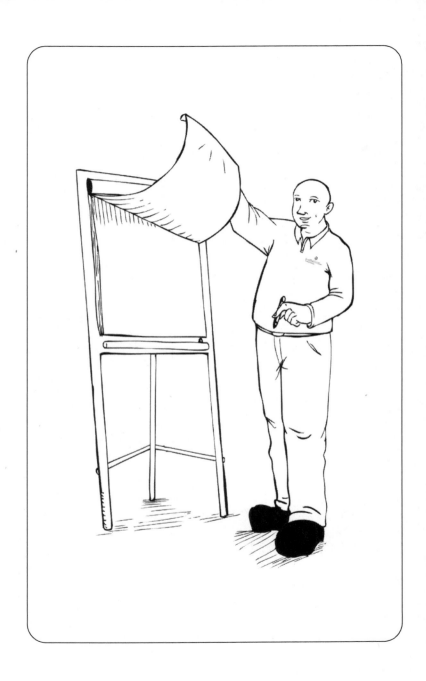

Chapter 3

Do you want Pain or Profit?

W HEN YOU LOOK at any successful company they do just a few things in some form or another in order to get and keep their business. Over the years I have identified what these things are - and there are only six key areas - but as tradesmen we tend to neglect most of them, or at best we do them all half-heartedly. So in this chapter I'll explain to you what these six key areas are and why you need to master all of these areas effectively.

Step 1

If you don't do this... you won't get the jobs you really want

Maybe you think that you need to take on any job in any area in order to keep a steady stream of customers coming to you. Because of this you possibly spend a great deal of time working outside of your local area meaning a lot of your working week is taken up with travelling. Perhaps you think if you offer just one type of service you will get fewer customers.

But what if I tell you that when you fail to define what it is that you do, the type of work you want and you don't target specific customers or areas (but hope that everyone will be your clients) you actually hinder your chances of getting the work that you really want? I often tell my trainees...

"When you look for everyone you get no-one"

Wouldn't it be great to only work with the clients you really want to, doing the specific line of work you love to do, and, all within an easy reach of your business premises?

To achieve this in your business you must Specialise.

Step 2

If you don't do this... people will not consider you an expert

Perhaps you have been fishing in the same pond as every other electrician. Maybe you've been saying the same things as all the other tradesmen out there and your business even looks very similar to the next one.

When you look at successful companies or individuals they stand out as experts in their field. You don't need to be gimmicky or outrageous to achieve this expert status.

Over the years I have found that most people still sometimes have a negative perception of tradesmen. They are expecting you to walk through the door and go "ooh that'll cost you missus!" Years ago electricians were held to a higher standard, but in recent years that has deteriorated and this might be due to the sheer number of people now entering the industry. It has become a little easier for people to enter into the trade these days through shorter training courses or a domestic installer course for example. I am not saying these are bad; it's just that some do have this as their way into the industry.

Sadly 'the public' have formed opinions of what tradesmen are. They are never sure if they will be ripped off, nor can they be certain of the skill level of a particular tradesman. So you must find ways of combatting this and build a level of trust with your potential customer before they make their buying decision. Instil in your potential customer a level of confidence that makes them absolutely certain that they have the right guy before they buy.

Wouldn't it be great if your customer knew beyond any shadow of a doubt that you were an expert in your field and that they could trust you? Better still that when they choose you as the one to do the job they are certain they won't be ripped off or left in a worse situation than when they started. Even better still is having customers seek you out for your expertise, rather than you having to go looking for them.

---

*To achieve this, the key thing is **Positioning***

Step 3

If you don't get this right... you will simply be throwing money away

Perhaps up until now you have advertised when you need the work or when things slow down, or maybe you do actually advertise regularly but often it's only because you got a deal on the rate or someone told you this was the thing to do.

I imagine you have produced flyers and brochures at some point as this is generally where everyone starts, but it shouldn't necessarily be your starting point. If you went down this route then you were simply copying what went before you and doing the same things everyone else has done. Chances are although you may be getting some work your results are likely to be poor and sporadic.

As tradesmen we are susceptible to ad companies calling us and telling us they will get our brand or business in front of thousands of homeowners, so we spend money with them promoting our business, but, is it getting the result we want? Do we even know just how effective it is (or not as the case may be). The reality is you most likely don't know how effective it's been.

You might also have considered spending money with a lead generation company, or maybe you paid to become a member and subsequently paid for leads they sent your way. Now, what they don't tell you is that when you sign up is that they also sell 'your lead' to other electricians, so your potential customer will also have got other electricians to quote as well that were sent from the lead gen company, plus they may even have approached others independently. It has cost your potential customer nothing, but it's cost you to get the lead and to travel there to do the quote and then, after all that, you may never even get the work!

Wouldn't it be great if you really understood how to make advertising effective rather than just copying what everyone else does? Wouldn't you like to know exactly what works and what doesn't work for you and your business and ultimately keep your diary filled month after month after month!

---

*So the thing you need to get right here is **A**dvertising*

Step 4

If you don't do this… winning repeat business will be difficult

Maybe you do have some repeat business coming in, but my guess is you possibly still have to advertise to get most of your customers. Perhaps you don't know how to control getting repeat business and recommendations or maybe someone has told you 'you can't have friends in business.'

Most tradesmen will go and do the job, cash the cheque and then that is the end of the connection with the customer.

I realised that there are many companies out there that are excelling by making their customer feel reliant upon them and although our industry is not the same as a bank or supplier of utilities for example, you can still create the same kind of feeling of rapport and community with your customer.

Who are the people we depend on most in our lives? It's generally our friends, right? Friends are loyal, trusting and want to see you do well. So my thought was if I could make my customers feel more than just a customer, if I could convert my customers into friends, even distant friends, in a managed way then they would trust me, be loyal to me and depend on me when they had a need I knew how to fix.

Wouldn't it be great if your customer considered you a friend and your name was on speed dial in their phone? Better still that because you are now their 'brilliant electrician friend' that they tell everyone else about you.

So the thing to concentrate on here is Relationships

Step 5

If you don't do this... you will be forever chasing new customers

You may have thought that if you contact a customer regularly that they will get fed up hearing from you and any effort you make will be wasted. And this can be true if you don't do it properly. Or perhaps you have considered sending regular emails or newsletters of some kind but have no idea what to put in them. Or maybe you are like 99% of all other trades that never give the customer a second thought once the cheque has been cashed.

No matter how much other business you have - a repeat customer is always cheaper than any other customer you could get. Every new customer will cost you something, either time, money, or both. A repeat customer doesn't cost you anything and if they bring their friends and family to you, even better!

Communication is one area that most tradesmen fall down on in a big way, and that is in all forms, from keeping appointments, sending written quotes, reconnecting after quoting, project information, and long term follow up after a job has been completed. Many tradesmen just don't see the point in doing any of this and have a mindset of 'if they need me, they will contact me.'

What you ought to be doing is making sure again that you are the one they think of when they want work done. It's about keeping you in the forefront of their mind for certain jobs. There are a number of simple ways in which you can keep your name and brand in front of your customers without them unsubscribing or putting you in the recycling pile!

Imagine sending your customers a newsletter and getting an email from them thanking you for the information you sent them. Wouldn't it be great if not only do they tell you how very useful it was to hear from you at that particular time but they could actually do with you going round to do some work.

---

*So you need to master the art of **K**eeping in Touch*

Step 6

If you don't do this… you could end up with a diary that's feast one month and famine the next

It's possible that until now you hadn't grasped the difference between advertising and marketing and so perhaps you have taken the ad hoc approach to placing adverts as and when you needed the work. Maybe you have never used a proper marketing calendar or have no idea what resources you have available to you and you've possibly experienced the 'feast or famine' stages that often plague us tradesmen.

Most of us go from day to day, week to week and month to month doing nothing actively to get and keep customers. We hope people will refer us but have nothing in place to ensure it happens.

I've said before that *'If you don't have customers you don't have a business'* and so you really MUST dedicate some of your time to getting and keeping customers. By not doing this you will end up spending more on your advertising and marketing and letting lots of money go - so, in effect, you end up treading water. There is no such thing as standing still in business, you are either moving forward or backward. You should maximise the amount of money you are getting from each customer. Have you ever considered what the lifetime value of a customer is to you?

To get to the bottom of this you need to have something in place that helps you cost effectively find new customers on a regular basis so that you don't have to look, day in day out, for new prospects. You need to implement something that provides you with a funnel of new prospects, which means you can cherry pick the kind of work you want to do from the prospects that you have coming in.

Wouldn't it be great to have a system in place whereby you always have a steady flow of work to fill your diary? Better still it only takes you 60 minutes a day and doesn't cost you anything to ensure that this happens.

---

*What I am talking about here is **S**ystemising*

The S.P.A.R.K.S. Blueprint™ addresses all SIX of these areas and demonstrates how easy it is to implement a few changes in the way you market your business that will ensure you can keep your diary filled month after month.

Mindset

Before getting into the six steps of the S.P.A.R.K.S. Blueprint™ it is important to ensure that you are approaching your marketing with the right mindset.

---

*"If you keep doing what you're doing,
you will keep getting what you're getting"*

The first mind shift that you need to make is to understand that you must dedicate time to marketing your service. There is often confusion about the relationship between marketing and advertising. Advertising alone is not marketing, yet many tradesmen believe that placing a few ads is all the marketing that they need to do.

From the day you open for business, marketing for your trades-based business consists of "everything you do and everything you say" as the author Regis McKenna stated. That is to say marketing is not just something you do when work is short, marketing needs to be considered in every aspect of your business. As a sole trader or small company, you are your brand and as such you need to be putting out a consistent and congruent image of your business.

The second mind shift that you need to make is this...getting customers is more important than the actual job you do! As tradesmen we are very proud of the work we do, we spend a lot of time and money honing our skills and we invest in the best tools to do the job. We will often openly brag about how well versed in the regulations we are, but none of this holds any value if we don't stay in business. To stay in business we need customers, good customers, paying customers and preferably returning customers. We need to learn how to get these customers and keep them and we need to dedicate a small portion of every day to do this, instead of just putting our head down and getting on with the work.

Mind shift number three is that we need to stop competing and start dominating. This is actually much easier than it would first appear. Competing causes us to focus on what everyone else in our market is doing so we then try to outdo one another; bigger advert, more sponsorship, bigger spend on web presence and lower prices than the competition - but all of this sets you up for failure. By simply copying what others are doing but 'bigger' is not going to help you get more customers. If it's not effective for your competition, then why would it be effective for you? If you are reducing your price to compete remember there will always be someone who is prepared to be cheaper - don't be that person.

Instead become the dominant electrician in your area. You need to be the name on the tip of everyone's tongue when someone needs what you do. You need to be so dominant in your local area that they don't even consider anyone else. Once you define your niche (which I'll talk about later), this is actually not difficult to achieve.

What do you think of when I say burger, training shoe or pizza?

These are simple examples I know but I bet for each of these you had only one or two brand names come to mind and if you had two you still had a dominant one. This is the type of reaction you want in your local area when people want an electrician, a new consumer unit or an electrical inspection for example. Your aim is to ensure that it is your name that comes to mind. Not only is this achievable but you can also have your name prominent when they need other trades as well and we will discuss the value of this in a later chapter.

At this point you're possibly thinking to yourself there's a lot going on here and it might seem a bit overwhelming to you, you may even feel that there is too much to do on your own, or that you're not good enough at marketing or you will never be able to find the time to do all this...

...Don't panic!

The following chapters will break it down for you step by step.

You don't have to do everything all at once but by accepting that you need to focus on your marketing you can start by introducing just one small thing at a time. As each new thing is in place, simply add another one. By adding each bit incrementally you are way more likely to take this step and start to make very positive changes in your business.

ToolBox tales...

I came across James and The ToolBox on Facebook. I was thinking of closing my business at the time due to not having a steady flow of work and a stable income.

James was holding a ToolBox talk in Ireland and I felt I had nothing to lose by attending. Best decision I have ever made for my business as James knew all about the struggles of being self employed and trying to run a business.

Most especially, he understood how hard it is to succeed in the electrical trade and with his guidance and support my business has been going from strength to strength.

James is always there for advice whenever you need him and his private Facebook page is great for getting feedback from fellow ambitious electricians and from James himself.

Since I have joined I have gone from having a days work here and there to filling up my dairy with jobs I enjoy doing and all with James's marketing techniques to help my business grow.

It's well worth the money for his guidance and support only regret I have is that I didn't find him sooner.

Stephen Power
Power Electrical

Specialise

"Everyone is not your customer…"
Seth Godin

Chapter 4

The **S**pecialist Niche Generator

BEING AN ELECTRICIAN (or indeed any trade) can mean that you have a vast array of skills to call upon, and this is a good thing when it comes to doing the work that we do. Unfortunately it is not such a good thing when we are marketing our services, because most tradesmen seem to list everything that they are capable of doing and cast their net so wide that they are seen as generalists and not as specialists. Generalists are 'two to a penny' and the guy who does everything is undervalued as a jack of all trades.

When you specialise you can easily dominate a sector of your market, niching is the term given to creating a small segment of a much bigger market and this is exactly what you need to do. The way I look at it is that you have a better chance of survival by being a big fish in a very small pond than you have by being a small fish in the ocean.

In order to effectively niche your business, there are three areas in which you need to claim your space:

- **What** - What do you do well? What do you enjoy doing?

- **Who** - Who is your ideal customer? Who values what it is that you offer?

- **Where** - How far do you really want to travel for work? What will you define as local?

What?

The first thing you need to do, that most of us don't do, is to define what we want to offer in the way of a service. Yes, we are electricians, but as you and I know that covers a broad spectrum. We need to define ourselves as the type of electrician we are within our trade. Each of us will be capable of a full range of electrical work, yet there will be areas that we all have that hold a special interest. For example some will enjoy 'house bashing' while others will enjoy replacing consumer units or fault finding and yet others will prefer working on new builds and conversely will have areas or aspects of the work that they dislike or don't find profitable.

Doesn't it make sense then to promote the work you want and find profitable and build your business around that?

The reason people don't do this is that they are afraid that if they promote themselves in only one area they will lose work in others areas; yet the truth is very different. If you promote in one area and one sector of the industry it is much easier to build a reputation as being the guy who does 'that thing', which makes it easier for people who want 'that thing' done to find you, therefore you end up getting more work doing 'that thing'. Now if 'that thing' is what you want to be doing because you enjoy it or find it profitable or both, then doesn't it make sense that you should fill your diary based on 'that thing'?

For example: - if you were to become known as the sparks who specialises in consumer unit changes and you had a diary full of consumer unit changes would it matter that people didn't ask you to do rewires? Of course not! But, by the way, they will ask anyway! The fear that they won't is an irrational one, because even though you promote a specialist skill people will still ask you to do other work.

If you have fifteen electricians in your local area but you become the guy that's recognised as the guy that specialises in rewires then you are way more likely to get all or at least most of the house rewiring projects, because you have become the 'go-to guy' for house rewires.

So niche down and figure out what it is that you actually want to do in terms of what you do and then promote that. Does that mean you don't do any other work? No! It just means that in terms of your marketing it's much more targeted. And if your marketing is targeted at the stuff that you want to do then what will happen is that you will get more of what it is that you are looking for.

---

*"Nothing is really work unless you would rather be doing something else." - **James M. Barrie***

Describe your ideal type of work, what do you enjoy doing that is profitable for you?

- .

- .

- .

- .

- .

Who?

Once you know what it is you are offering, you then need to decide who you want to offer it to. Ask any electrician who is his potential customer and the answer you are likely to get is *"anyone"*, because at some time everyone needs or will need an electrician. Yet are all customers equal? I don't believe they are. We all have customers that have been a nightmare to work for, we have all had some who have just been okay and yet others that have been a real pleasure to work for and yet when we look for work we spread a net and we think everyone is our customer.

You are just happy when the phone rings and the customer asks if you can you come and do a quote for this or that. I believe that's the wrong approach - you should be targeting the type of customers for what you want. Not every customer is a good one!

Have you ever gone to a customer and wished you had never ever taken on the job!?

It's not the job that's the problem, it's the person you are doing the job for. But if you niche who it is you actually want to work for it will make your life so much easier and get you the customer that you ideally want. Creating an ideal customer profile provides you with a lot of useful marketing information. Large companies do this very well and it is a trick I believe that smaller companies and sole traders are missing out on.

Let us look at a profile for one of my ideal customers for example - Mary is a 45 year old, 'stay at home' housewife with a husband called John who works in the city and commutes long hours every day. She drives a four door family car, has two kids a boy 12 and a girl 14 and she lives with them all in a well-kept 1930's house. Mary looks after herself, goes to the gym regularly, attends the local hairdresser and dotes on her kids - who she regularly takes off to their extracurricular events.

How do I know that this is a good profile for my ideal customer? It's simply because I go back through all of my customer data (we all keep our records right?) and strip out all the information I can about the people I have previously done business with, that I enjoyed working for, that paid well and that didn't cause any problems. I then collate that information and add a bit of wishful thinking, this then gives me the characteristics that make up my profile; I then give her or him a name, in this case Mary.

So what is the value in doing this?

Now when I write an advert or prepare a letter for a promotion I have a picture of Mary in my mind. This makes it easier to target my promotion at my ideal customer because I can speak their language, touch their pain & pleasure points and answer the objections that I know they will have. So, I know how to write my adverts and where to target my marketing because now I am not talking or trying to appeal to 'everyone'. Not only am I now talking to Mary but by defining who she is I now know where to place my ads! It gives me a picture of what she likes doing and where she goes each week. If she takes kids to karate every week then there is value in me sponsoring an event there.

If she goes to the hairdressers every month and spends about £60 each time then it could be worth me doing a joint venture with the hairdresser as I know that other clients there may well need me at some point and I can promote the hairdresser in return.

"I am grateful for all the awkward and pedantic customers I have ever had, they have shown me who I don't want to work for." - **James Dewane**

This doesn't mean you don't take work in from anyone else, it just means that you get more of the work you want and with the people you want to work with by doing this kind of marketing.

There is great value in sitting down and working out who your ideal customer is…

Write a few lines that describe who your ideal customer is…

- -

- -

- -

- -

- -

- -

- -

Where?

Now we know the 'what' and the 'who' all that remains is to work out the 'where'. Based on my own history I was originally happy to travel anywhere. If there's money there I would go and do it whether London, Birmingham or anywhere else there was work. My mantra was I'll follow the money.

The reality is that excessive travel for tradesmen can be a false economy, we went into business to make money - for independence and to better our standard of living. Travelling four hours a day in the van is not doing anything to better our standard of living! And, often we can lose money on what we think is a worthwhile project but by the time you add up fuel, food, accommodation, time on the road, delays due to traffic etc. it's often not worth it and that's before you start to resent the journey which in turn affects your mood, that in turn effects how you relate to others; not great!

So I came to the realisation that if I could dominate an area (geographically) then I don't have to travel miles.

You can literally put a circle of 15 - 20 miles around the area you are based (assuming you are in a reasonably populated area and not 10 miles from the nearest civilisation) and find your customers within that. You really do not need to travel far to find good work.

If you dominate the market in your local area, you really can generate enough work to support you, your business, your family and whatever you want. I used to do the travel thing,

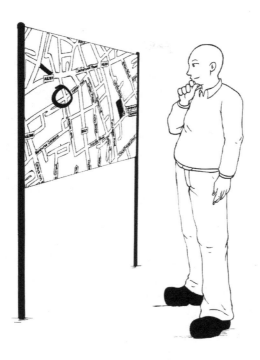

but using this model and by being the name on the tip of people's tongues in my area my phone barely stopped ringing.

"Travel is to be enjoyed and should be for pleasure not for work." - ***James Dewane***

It's so easy for anyone prepared to step up and stick their head above the parapet to become that person in their area. There's so many tools you can use now to do this; the web, social media, webinars, video, etc. but incredibly no one is doing it yet.

When you're the one that's blogging, writing articles for the papers, magazines and websites and on the local radio with helpful hints and tips etc. whose name do you think will be top of their mind when they think local electrician? Of course, it will be yours.

Understanding the What, Who and Where means that you can now make your marketing efforts much more targeted. Knowing what work you are looking for, who you want to work for and where you want to limit that search for work is going to ensure that you spend your time doing more of the type of work you want to do. It also means that you now have a niche in which you can begin to position yourself as the expert.

How far do you want to travel for work, mileage from base of operations?

- -

- -

- -

I received an email from James explaining what he does…

I get 10 to 15 emails a day selling me things.

James' email talked to me as a person/and electrician so something the other hundred companies failed to do so I gave him a go.

I recommend James because he delivers on so many levels, he is a font of marketing knowledge, and he and his colleagues offer good technical advice. And the Electricians ToolBox is full of great tips.

There are business consultants out there who charge thousands of pounds for less than James delivers. I have increased my business by 20% by applying just some of James' tips.

Enough said.

Nigel Rooney
Herts and Beds Electrical
www.rooneyelectrical.co.uk

Positioning

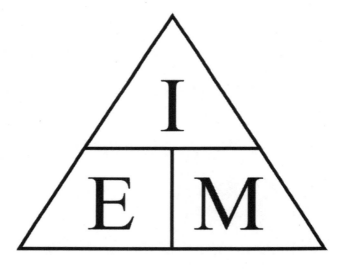

"You are already an expert at what you do, you simply have to broadcast it now so everyone else knows it too…"
James Dewane

Chapter 5

The Expert **P**ositioning Pyramid

THE MAJORITY OF tradesmen will have spent at least three years on an apprenticeship and maybe also done some CPD (Continuing Professional Development) and no doubt had to join industry bodies and buy industry related journals. These are all things that experts have in common and must invest in, yet we as electricians have allowed ourselves to be commoditised.

Expert positioning is so important for a number of reasons, firstly people don't haggle with or question experts, plus they will value and are willing to pay a premium for those they consider to be an expert, for example a lawyer, surgeon and even a pilot. I firmly and honestly believe that we deserve that status also, after all we study hard to qualify and we often jump through hoops to remain current and on top of industry and legislative changes.

For too long now we have been looked at as a commodity - like a loaf of bread or a pint of milk - and with that goes the thinking that you shouldn't need to pay more for a commodity. We have to change this and make sure that people now see us as the experts we truly are.

What you need to understand is
"You're already an expert, you just have to let people know it"

Let me tell you a story. One of my hobbies is scuba diving, now I know that Crete isn't known as a scuba destination for the skilled diver, however when you understand that I am not a thrill seeker when it comes to diving, no wrecks, caves, or fish bigger than myself. For me it's a bit like advanced snorkelling, not too deep, nice shallow waters and I watch the fish.

For this story I'm going to take you on holiday with me, and we're on a beach on the north east coast of Crete. The sun is baking the golden sand, most of the tourists are sheltering under the great rows of Cretan palms that grow on the beach. We're just laying on the sand soaking in the sun.

"I fancy a dive - are you up for it?"

"Yeah go on then, why not, I'll give it a go" you reply.

We stand up and walk down the beach and can see two scuba stalls. One has Costas smoking a fag in his string vest and flip flops with a bit of scribbled paper stuck to his stall that says 45 Euros per dive. As we get closer to the stalls we see that Costas has what would just about pass for a boat, it seems to be wooden framed and looks like it's been patched up and has a couple of old sun bleached buoys hanging over the edge.

On the other side we have Yani at his stall - he actually looks like a sailor, nice navy polo shirt, white trunks, company logo and his stand is beautifully wrapped with photos of people that have been on dives. He looks well organised and is standing there encouragingly with his lovely white branded yacht behind him. His sign also states 45 Euros per dive.

Now, you have never been on a scuba dive before and given that they both cost the same - which way do you think we are going to go?

Well, let me add that Yani has a queue of people wanting to go with him, and Costas is standing alone...does that help you decide?

Okay, I know you want to go with Yani but I head over to Costas. Now the reason I head to Costas is because I've been going to him almost every year for the last sixteen years and he knows the waters off this coast, he is very safety conscious, understands the weather and the currents, knows the best dive sites and to the best of my knowledge has

never had any incidents, **he is most definitely an expert**, but, everyone else seems to favour Yani.

This is the first time in sixteen years that I have seen Yani, I know nothing about him and neither do the queue of people who are standing in line waiting to put their life in his hands. So why is he so busy?

Well, as you will most likely have realised by now, Yani has the best marketing. He looks like an expert!

Who is doing that to you? Who in your line of work is eating your lunch and taking your business because they look the part? They may not be as skilled as you, they may not be as conscientious or as honest as you, but in the eyes of the public they look like the expert and it's all because they are good at marketing themselves.

How would things change if you start to take control of your marketing, show people your expertise and position yourself locally as the expert? The beauty of it is that it's not difficult to do and there are only three things you need to understand and make use of to create your expert status.

1 - CREATE AN IMAGE

They say you never get a second chance to make a first impression, but when do you make that first impression - when the phone rings? When you arrive to do a quote? When you turn up to do a job and knock on the door - is that when a customer forms their first impression of you? Or is the first impression when they see your advertising - or when you get recommended?

None of the above: you need to understand that it's the day you open the door to your business.

From that first day you are creating an impression, now you have got to decide are you going to control what that impression is or are you just going to hope that people form a good impression of you?

You don't know when someone is looking at or judging you, you don't know when a potential customer is looking at your advert, checking your social media profile, spots you out in your van or sees you out on the town for an evening. You are the image of your company, and you need to be aware of the affect of your actions on that image. You just never know who's watching when you get angry at being cut up in the van and offer the one finger salute, or who is reading your Facebook or Twitter posts when you air your views!

If you want to be taken seriously as an expert in your field then you need to manage your image. If you give off the wrong image it won't matter how great you are as a tradesman, people will judge you by the impression they form, long before they actually meet you.

2 - EDUCATE

When you educate others you demonstrate your expertise, you may be thinking "I'm not a teacher - how would I educate". The thing is you have knowledge that others don't, you know how to do things that others don't, and you may even have picked up some great simple ways of doing things that others aren't aware of! Then you have people who want to know how to do some simple things, like how to rewire a plug-top, while others don't fully understand how their consumer unit works or maybe want to know what's involved in wiring a house. By teaching that stuff - even if it seems simple to you - it positions you as an expert.

Have you ever gone out to a customer and tried to explain something; perhaps what the earthing system is, but you can't get them to understand why you can't do the work until the system is updated, or maybe you've tried to explain the difference between old wired fuses and new MCBs.

If you can hand them a simple explanation on a piece of branded paper that helps incredibly. It helps them to simply take in the information and assists in positioning you as an expert.

So, what if you wrote blogs on simple DIY skills or created simple explanatory videos? It doesn't have to be perfect because you are an electrician, not an Oscar winning actor and your audience won't be expecting polished videos. But, what they can benefit from is quality information put across in a reasonably good way.

How many tradesmen in your town are doing this type of thing now? My guess is none.

Where would that position you if you were the one doing it?

3 - MEDIA

Throughout our lives we are programmed to believe that anyone we see interviewed or commenting on a topic on the telly or radio is an expert! We assume, that if they are on there, they know what they are talking about and they have experience.

The same can be said of printed media. If we read a magazine article or a column in a newspaper we assume that it has been written by an expert in that particular field, or if it is not written by one certainly the content is the result of an interview with an expert in the field.

In order to broadcast your expert status you need to be making good use of all available media. Yes it may be difficult to get on the telly (not impossible), but you have YouTube and Vimeo; also you can post videos onto Facebook and Twitter.

So why don't more people do YouTube? It's usually because they think it's hard or too difficult. Truth is it's actually quite easy and not very expensive at all. I got my camera for £30 on eBay and the software I use to edit was $45 online and it's plenty good enough for what I want to do. Having said that if you have a smart phone then the camera on that is more than adequate and there is plenty of free editing software available online.

What's going to happen when your YouTube video goes up on how to install garden lighting? Mr Smith goes on to YouTube searching to see how to do that - and he finds your video. So who do you think he is he going to call when he realises that it's not a small job?

You can target your videos to your local area so that the people who find them will be local to you, if you have done it right.

People don't approach their local radio station because they think it will be expensive to advertise or hard to get a slot, but actually the truth is local radio stations have to give over a lot of their air time to local stories and events and they have to fill them with local content. If you can provide them with that content chances are they will jump at the chance and be pleased to talk with you.

The same can be true for local newspapers, free papers and magazines. If you can provide them with regular content then you basically have free advertising by simply placing your contact details at the end of every article you submit. The key to doing this is to make the articles relevant to the target audience; for example you could create DIY articles and articles discussing how changes in the industry affect the reader, or you could offer some safety tips. The key thing is not to attempt to sell - this is about you creating your expert position, it is not about selling your services.

I provide members of My Electricians ToolBox™ with new articles every month, they simply have to alter them for their own local market and put their own branding on them. Not only can you download my tip sheet for creating articles, but also get my free training on creating YouTube videos at **www.jdewane.com/gifts**

The great thing about creating articles for publication is that you can use the same article in a number of different ways on a number of different types of media. Let's say I write a brief 500 word article on the benefits of converting to LED lighting - I can submit it to a local magazine, a local newspaper and post it on my blog. The same article can then be broken into shorter sections and posted on my Facebook page with links back to the full article on my blog, likewise with my Twitter account I can tweet one liners and link back to the blog. I can also use the content of the article to create a video. So you see it doesn't have to be hard, complicated or time consuming yet the benefits of building your expert position speak for themselves.

By doing this you are putting yourself way ahead of your competition. You will get to a point where your local customers will say "I want that guy! I've seen his videos, I've read his articles and I heard him on the radio recently and he knows what he is talking about - he's the one I want!"

"The public do not know enough to be experts in your field, but they know enough to decide which expert to call and that expert should be you!" - **James Dewane**

Awareness

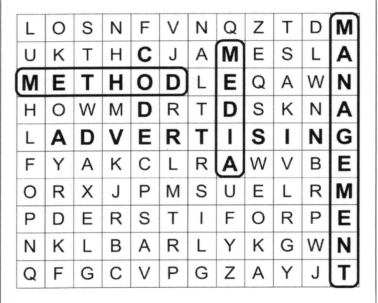

"You can be the best electrician in the world, but you won't make any money unless people know about you."
James Dewane

Chapter 6

The Local **A**dvertising Code

PEOPLE OFTEN CONFUSE marketing with advertising – advertising is only one part of the marketing mix, however, it is an important part. If people don't know you exist they can't use your service and if they don't know what you do or how to contact you then they are never going to be your customer.

If you crack The Local Advertising Code then you can have a funnel of work coming in. Remember, advertising doesn't have to be expensive, in fact, it shouldn't cost you anything. Every time you spend money on advertising you should get a return, therefore it is an investment not an expense – or at least it is if you do it right.

Imagine an old one arm bandit machine...you remember the type, you put a coin in the top pull the handle, the tumblers would turn and how they landed decided how much you won. Well what would happen if you found such a machine and every time you put a £1 coin in it gave you back 5 x £1 coins? When would you stop putting coins in?

Unfortunately what happens is that we as tradesmen don't invest enough time and effort into finding the one arm bandit, instead we copy what everyone else is doing. If the sparks down the road is advertising in the local paper then we think we should. If he has a banner in the golf club then we follow suit. The problem with this is we have no idea if it is working for him, so how do we know if it will work for us? We look through other peoples adverts and copy the same layout without giving any thought to whether it even works as an advert let alone appeals to our 'ideal client'.

Vanity advertising afflicts most small business owners as we have this need for significance; a need to see our name or our business name in print. You need to understand that your customer is not looking for you specifically, I am sorry to say, but it's true. They are looking for a solution of some sort, a solution to some form of problem; they are looking for what it is they need. They do not know you, your company or your logo at this point. All they want to know is "Who is going to solve my problem?"

So if it's an electrician they are after it will be the word ELECTRICIAN that will catch their attention not James Dewane & Sons or Medway Property Maintenance.

Consider the brain to act a little like Google in this sense, if you were searching for local swimming lessons you wouldn't type in … 'John Dempsey Swimming Instructor'… you would be more likely to type in … 'Swimming Lessons' or 'Local

Swimming Lessons'... Your advertising should do the same. Your company name and logo do have a place in your business and in creating your image but advertising is about getting the phone to ring. I would rather have a simple and effective ad that got my phone ringing than a fancy well branded ad that did nothing.

I encourage the electricians I work with to get rid of this idea that your logo or your name is the most important thing. The most important thing is that customers can see how you can solve their problem or give them a solution. Once they have contacted you, once they pick up the phone or send an email, then you can impress them with your graphics and clever company name, but you must get them to take that first step.

If you only did this one thing, it would make a huge difference to the enquiries you get, simply because customers are looking for a solution and the answer to what they actually want. They are not looking for you!

Regardless of the type of advertising you are doing, there are only three components to The Local Advertising Code:

1 – Method

The method I follow is a version of the AIDA principle, a variation called AIDCA. The acronym stands for:-

Attention – **I**nterest – **D**esire – **C**redibility – **A**ction

Using the AIDCA model will help you ensure that any kind of writing, whose main purpose is to get the customer to do something, is as effective as possible. First it must grab the target audience's attention, and engage their interest. Then it must build a desire for your service offering and create trust by demonstrating credibility, before setting out how to take the action that you want the audience to take.

Attention - get the customers attention

You are never going to force people to buy something they don't need, well at least not in our industry, unlike the retail sector where people often make impulse purchases. So your aim is to draw attention to your advert in such a way that the potential customer will remember you when they need your service, it's not to get them to make an instant purchase. Psychology can play a big part in this, for example, did you know that a newspaper advert with a hashed line around it will get a better response that one with a solid line (assuming everything else in the advert is identical).

The reason is that over many years our brains have become attuned to a hashed line being something to cut out, such as a coupon, and so our eyes are drawn to simply check it out. It doesn't guarantee a response as after all the reader may not want an electrician, but, this simple tactic gets attention and is only one of hundreds of ways to draw people to your advert including the use of colour, contrast, fonts, the location of an advert and the method of delivery.

Interest - you have to pique the customer's interest

Let's assume now that your advert has got their attention, now you want them to read the advert, you need to create some interest. It's great that you have diverted their eyes away from other adverts and distractions but now you want them to see what you're offering. This is done by appealing directly to the potential customer's needs & wants and is a great example of why you need to define your ideal customer.

Often at this point adverts go wrong because the writer believes that what is important to them is important to the customer, it's not, your customer won't care that you have been in business sixty five years or that you have qualifications from XYZ university, at least not at this point. This is where you need to be inside your customers head and think what is important to them.

Desire - make it desirable to them

Why should they pick up the phone and call you and not the guy in the next advert? When you know your ideal customer you have a better chance of making yourself appear desirable to them. This may be in the form of an offer they can't resist, it may simply be something about the way you do business, where you're located or it may simply be what it is you specialise in.

The Interest and Desire parts of the AIDCA model can go hand-in-hand, but while you're building the reader's interest, you also need to help them understand how what you're offering can help them in a real way. The main way of doing this is by appealing to their personal needs and wants.

Credibility - show them they can trust you

Often a big issue with customers looking for tradesmen is the trust factor. "Are they going to overcharge me? Are they going to do poor work? Are they really qualified?" The more fears you can put to rest at the advertisement stage the more likely your advert will get a response. If you are registered with an awarding body then state it, in fact put their logo on your advert, the fact is that their logo will be more recognisable than yours.

Action - encourage them to take action

Never just put your number on the advert and assume that the customer will use it, tell them what to do, make sure it is clear how you want them to respond. Literally put 'pick up the phone' or 'email me'. People do tend to follow instructions. Now, again you need to remember if they don't need an electrician at the time of reading the ad they are not likely to respond, however, you are appealing to those who do need you. There is one call to action that I have used on leaflets to great effect and that is simply "KEEP THIS FLYER HANDY UNTIL YOU NEED A LOCAL ELECTRICIAN". If your target is local, that is to say you are after local work, then adding your name to the call to action also has a great effect. For example, "Call James on..." rather than simply "Call..." Or "Call Us..."

Exercise: Using AIDCA as a guide draw an advert you feel will work for your business…

A well-structured advertisement is key. This was my all-time best performing advert, it performed so well in magazines and papers that I adopted a version of it for leaflets.

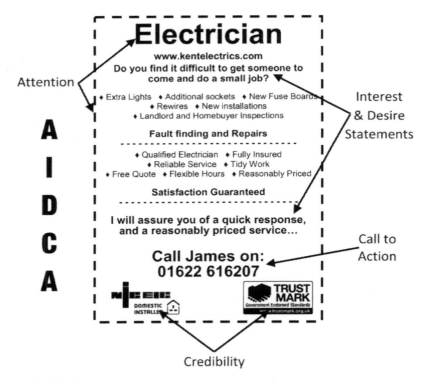

2 – Media

There are many different forms of media available for us to advertise in as local business people; newspapers, directories, local magazines, flyers, leaflets, the web, social media, sponsorship deals, club banners, hoardings, A frames, shops signage, your van etc. The list goes on and on. So why is it that we tend to do the same thing over and over?

Yes, when we start we may do a small bit of leafleting, try some networking and post an ad in the yellow pages, but very soon we get stuck in a rut of doing the same one or two things over and over again, we get comfortable.

The thing is not only are we oblivious to whether our advertising is working or not (more about that in a moment), but we do the same ad the same way in the same place over and over and don't realise that there is such a thing as 'advertising blindness'. There are several reasons for 'ad blindness'. Even if a person is staring at the ad, it might not register in their mind because it has been seen so many times before - it's a bit like driving home and not remembering anything about the journey, you are so used to it you just tuned out.

I do not recommend that as a small business you should try every form of advertising all the time, but I do believe you should try a number of different forms, change from time to time and test your results - which is what the third step, Management, is all about.

3 – Management

It was Henry Ford who said – *"I know at least half my advertising works, I just don't know which half"* and Einstein is widely reported as having said *"Insanity is doing the same thing over and over but expecting a different result"*

Now take a look at both of the statements above and consider what most tradesmen do when advertising. In most cases we have no idea what is working. We may have a feeling or a sense that one advert or promotion is working. We might even try to keep records of where each call came from, but often other things take priority, for example, if you are a sole trader taking your own calls, you may intend to ask each caller how they got your details, you may intend to record that information on a spread sheet so that you can analyse it later. However, the truth is often that when the phone rings you are up to your neck in something and can barely get the details you need to call the person back, then when you do call them back you don't remember to ask how or where they got your details. The result is that advertising becomes guess work, so when it comes to renewing your advertising you don't know what is working and what isn't - so you simply renew and hope for the best.

I encourage the use of tracking numbers and tracking URLs as these are the most accurate way to manage your advertising and know what is and what isn't working. I use a company called Connect-It (www.connect-it.co) to provide me with local tracking numbers. The concept is quite simple and inexpensive. You simply purchase a series of local (virtual) numbers, these numbers all point at your main number, this can be your office or mobile. You use a different number for each advert / promotion, you then have an online portal (webpage) where you can log in and see your statistics, so you know how many calls a particular advert/promotion or leaflet received. This removes the guess work and gives you some very accurate statistics which can help you to make your advertising much more effective.

I have really simplified the tracking number explanation above because the system is capable of so much more. The use of virtual numbers means that you can work on the move providing people with landline numbers to ring but you pick up the calls on your mobile. They allow you to have a geographical presence in an area where perhaps you don't have an office (with a local number). You can configure the system to do any number of different things, like divert to your mobile if the office phone isn't answered, or call multiple members of staff at the same time (ensuring every call is answered).

Some people are wary of using tracking numbers because they are stuck in the past, where people remembered phone numbers and when phone numbers were associated with the organisations. I can assure you having used tracking numbers myself for the past seven years and working with electricians who are now doing the same, these fears are unfounded. Your main business number will remain your main number on your business cards, letterheads, invoices and quotes, you simply use tracking numbers on all of your advertising and promotions.

Employing this tactic will save you a small fortune in wasted advertising by pinpointing your most effective and least effective promotions, plus it will allow you to either alter your promotion or withdraw it completely.

If you would like more information on running leaflet campaigns that work you will find a full training membership that you can join for free at **www.jdewane.com/gifts**

Relationships

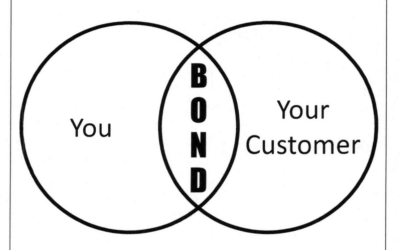

"You can make more friends in two months by becoming interested in other people, than you can in two years trying to get people to be interested in you."
Dale Carnegie

Chapter 7

The Relationship Accelerator

A NYONE WHO KNOWS anything about running a service based business, will tell you that getting repeat business or referred business is possibly the cheapest form of advertising you can do. There is an expense to getting every customer, but if that customer comes back to you then the cost of that customer gets less and less. If they bring their friends, family and colleagues then that in effect is free business.

Many tradesmen refer to this dismissively as word of mouth. Today you will still hear some say "most of my work is from word of mouth, I don't need to advertise" – yet very few tradesmen put any real effort into controlling their word of mouth marketing.

This chapter, and the next, focus on how you can take control of your word of mouth marketing and capitalise on every customer encounter. In this section we are going to look at how you start your relationship with the customer and in effect how you get someone to like you.

"People, like people like them" – James Dewane

Relationships are formed over a period of time, but there is usually something initially that brings two people together. Consider a man and woman who fall in love and decide to set up home together - the relationship is not formed immediately and in some cases it can take a considerable amount of time, while in others it can happen quite quickly. However, there is something that sparks enough interest to want to find out more, to become invested in working on a

relationship. This could be physical or sexual attraction, it could be his witty humour or her ability to understand the offside rule. Whatever it is there is always a starting point to any relationship, a point at which you want to know more or want to spend more time with the other person.

This phenomenon occurs naturally when we are in rapport with someone, however, you can take the chance element out of this and build rapport if you understand a few simple things about how the human brain works.

The first thing to understand is that you can make or break any relationship within the first few seconds of meeting someone, so, being aware of this you must take control of what happens at your first encounter. For many of us in the trade that first actual encounter will be when we turn up at the customers home to look at the potential work (to do the quote). You will have one set of goals or priorities (to get the job) and your potential customer will have their goals or priorities, but often the two don't match. Your potential customer may be wary of tradesmen, they may have had a bad experience or know someone who has had a bad experience, they may be intent on getting the lowest price (or at least think that's what they want). During this initial meeting most tradesmen are focused on the job in hand and not the person they are dealing with. Most will just want to get in, get the information to form the quote and then get out and on to the next job. The customer on the other hand may have a load of questions that they forget to ask, they may be inwardly concerned about showing you around their home, they will be listening for the stereotypical phrases that they have been told to expect like "oh that'll cost ya!" or "you don't want to do it that way" or "sorry mate we can't do that until you upgrade this, or sort out that..."

So, there is no rapport...

There's you on one side and your customer on the other and in order to build a relationship you need to find common ground, create a BOND and build rapport.

The Relationship Accelerator

There are four things you can do to accelerate creating rapport and these can be remembered using the acronym BOND. Your aim at an initial encounter is to get past any prejudice that your potential customer may have and to make them like you, so that when you leave they should be thinking how nice you were and how it would be great to work with someone like you, and not "well there goes another one let's see how expensive his quote will be.."

I am going to explain this now assuming your encounter is on the doorstep at the home of your potential client. You need to instantly create a **B O N D** and this can be achieved by doing the following...

B is for Banter - When you arrive don't be all about the job in hand. Your customer will be expecting you to behave in a certain way, they will expect to discuss the job and they may even expect that, like others, you will baffle them with technical language. So what you need to do is not show an immediate interest in the job, instead be interested in the person. I am not a psychologist nor do I profess to understand psychology in any deep and meaningful way, however if we accept what we have been told by psychologists for decades then we can agree on a number of facts.

- People like to hear their own name

- People like to talk about themselves

- People like to talk about things that interest them

- People like other people who show an interest in them and the things they like

So wouldn't it make sense then to talk in terms of what the customer is interested in? This is quite easy to work out with a little thought and imagination, evidence of a person's likes and potential personality are openly on display in and around their home.

For example:

The home itself - this was a judgement on the person's behalf, they decided to buy or build this particular type of house and they selected the neighbourhood.

The car on the drive - another personal decision. Is it fast and sporty, is it functional, and is there a loyalty to a brand?

How the garden is cared for - is it cared for? Has it been laid to concrete and tarmac or is it manicured lawns and nice flowers and shrubs?

Do they have pets and what type are they?

Do they have children, if so what age range and what are their interests?

Are there any interesting pictures or photographs on the wall?

All of the above, and more, with a little thought are great fuel for conversation, so rather than turn up and go straight into work mode, I would watch and observe as I turned up to the house.

Then, when they open the door they are not met with "Hi, I'm James, I'm here about the job." Instead they are met with "I see you have the new Lexus 4x4 hybrid. I've been looking at getting a new car and have been considering one of these myself. How do you like it?"

It gets you into a conversation that they are interested in.

If there are nice flowers and a manicured lawn - it means they care about the garden. If they have pets - do you think they care about them? Of course.

If you spot photographs on the wall depicting family or family days out, then that's important. There may be paintings, prints or photographs that reveal a hobby such as golf, rugby, flying or scuba; all areas that you can use as openers for some Banter.

Your aim is to get the customer talking about something that is of interest to them, and for you then to show interest in that topic. It is better if it is a genuine interest on your part rather than attempting to be false, so if you know nothing about gardens and care little for children or pets then these may not be the best topics to pick!

However if the household cat comes to say hello and you screw your nose up at it, what are they going to think? If you are being very dismissive of their children, they are not going to warm to you. Whether you like cats and children or not is irrelevant, you must make an effort to be friendly to them, because if the customer has them then they are important to the customer. I don't have a particular love for cats, I don't hate them I'm just not very fond of them, so if ever I have a situation where there is a cat getting a little too intimate (as they do) I simply tell the client that I love cats but unfortunately developed an allergy as I got older so they make my eyes and nose run. Far better than telling them I don't like cats.

O is for Observation – Ask questions, what do they actually want? What are their concerns, their fears? What are the signals they are giving off? Are they worried they can't trust you? Get to understand their real needs and wants, because if you know what their concern is, you can overcome it.

You see we tend to look at things on a surface level, so when the home owner tells us that they want a new socket installed in the bedroom or that they want a shower circuit installed, our mind goes to work solving that problem. You will most likely be thinking "how am I going to run the cable, is there enough capacity in the consumer unit, do I need to consider fitting an RCD?" When what the customer is thinking is "how long is it going to take, is my house going to be a wreck afterwards, do these guys have the right qualifications, what protection do I have if it all goes wrong or are they going to rip me off?"

You need to appreciate that what you see as being the problem may not be what the potential customer sees as the problem, so by being observant and asking relevant questions you can answer all of these fears and put them to rest in simple conversation.

N is for N.L.P – By using techniques from a practice called Neuro Linguistic Programming you can form strong relationships quickly with people by simply being like them. The more you can be like the person you want to build rapport with the more likely you are to get on with them. The more you are like someone, the more you are likely to be liked by them. Remember…*"People, like people like them."*

People mirror people they are in rapport with. Have you ever observed a group of two or more people in a social situation and noticed that they do something very similar very shortly after one another? For example, two ladies are out for a meal in a restaurant and you notice that when one crosses her legs the other follows suit, or two blokes chatting in a pub - one takes a swig of his drink the other does the same, or two executives talking after a meeting - one may loosen his tie and the other does exactly the same. These are basic examples of what is known in NLP as mirroring.

You can mirror body language, posture, tone of voice, and even breathing. These can be done either separately or in any combination. It is something that naturally occurs when people are in rapport and often it is so subtle that it goes unnoticed, but now that you are aware of it I bet you will notice it occurring much more often. NLP experts tell us that by using 'pacing', which is when you master the art of mirroring to the point that you can have your subject follow what you do, you can rapidly build rapport.

D is for being Decisive – or in NLP terms, future pacing, using positive and decisive language. Use presuppositions in your language, talk as if it was already a done deal, but without being cocky about it. So presuppose you are already doing the job. For example, say things like...

"When we get the contract...When I next see you...When we start, where do we park...? When we arrive, what is the earliest we can start?"

By saying 'if' you are saying you doubt you will get the job thereby putting doubt in their mind too and unconsciously giving them the option to choose between you and someone else.

Used correctly these tactics are great tools for building rapport with potential customers. Could they be abused? The simple answer is yes, and sadly they are abused by conmen and dodgy salesmen every day of the week. These people use these tactics to make sales and con people out of money but their success is short term. You, on the other hand, are honourable and well intentioned so you will use tactics like this to open what will be a lasting business relationship where you will give and add value to your customer's life, not simply take and run.

I am not an NLP Practitioner and my explanations of the principles are very basic and simply my interpretation from what I have learned over the years. If you plan to use any of these tactics I recommend you do some basic reading on the subject first. I can recommend **Unlimited Power** by *Anthony Robbins* or **Conversations with Richard Bandler** by *Owen Fitzpatrick*, both will give you a good basic understanding.

⌐ **ToolBox tales...** ───────────────

I was first contacted by James in an email he sent me regarding marketing for electricians. I had had previous emails from people regarding marketing but never found their emails very interesting and informative for my particular trade, they were very generalised.

I was intrigued to look into James' mail and his ideas as he was an electrician the same as me and it meant I would understand his methods more than general marketing ideas. I decided to join his ToolBox for a monthly subscription and as he had a no quibble money back guarantee, that meant if I didn't like it I could just walk away. (There is no contract to tie you in)

I admit I was sceptical as I had never seen a fellow tradesman giving this type of advice and didn't know what I was letting myself into. I needn't have worried, I can honestly say that the information I have received has been inspirational to me and exceeded all my expectations.

James gives you tried and tested advice and ideas, including documents inside the ToolBox that you can use and modify for yourself. The ToolBox is packed with loads of information that is released to you monthly so you don't get too overwhelmed all at once.

There are also live events for you to attend and meet up with like-minded trades people all looking to expand their business, and on top of that you also have a great day.

Since being a member of the ToolBox my sales have increased dramatically. I have gone from wondering where the next job was coming from on a weekly basis to being booked up to sometimes as far as three months in advance.

I think that being with the ToolBox is excellent value for money and would recommend it to any tradesmen/ women, not just electricians.

I would highly recommend the ToolBox to anyone wanting to increase their sales and expand their business to the next level.

Rob Cassie
RJCElectrics
www.rjc-electrics.co.uk

Keep in Touch

*"Without communication there is
no relationship…"*
Anon

Chapter 8

The Customer **K**eeper

WHEN YOU BUILD a relationship with someone you automatically build trust. Most tradesmen will view a relationship with a customer or potential customer as a transaction and as a result once the job is over and the cheque is cashed then the relationship is also over. If a customer has spent money with you then they trust you, at least to some degree, so wouldn't it make sense then to build on that trust?

We already know that the hardest thing in the buying cycle is getting the customer in the first instance. You will pay for a customer, whether through an advert, SEO, leaflets or banners etc. but once you have them, if you treat them properly they will come back to you time and time again. The problem is, most of us don't spend time in keeping the relationship going. If you simply keep in touch, your customer will come back time and again, but not only that, they will bring friends, family and colleagues.

How many times have you heard this...?

"Great job, really love the work you did
I'll always recommend you?"

Then you don't hear anything from them ever again. Why? What happens is, life gets in the way - they get on with other things, your business card gets misplaced or 'put away safely', your invoices have been binned, your phone number deleted from contact and so as time goes by you become a distant memory. Then, when someone eventually says to your old customer "I am getting some work done and need an electrician", that old customer replies "Oh we had a good one once, I think we got him from the magazine or maybe it was the web, now, what was his name? I wish I could remember."

What's even 'better' is when they eventually run into you again and tell you all about the job you nearly had because they nearly recommended you!

Wouldn't it be much better, and put your business in a different place, if when they are down the pub one of the guys says he's having work done on his property and your old customer is able to say "ah, you need to talk to James for that. He's the sparks that did a great job on mine 12 months ago, let me give you his contact details. I tell you what, we're still in touch so I'll get him to give you a call."

They will do that because you have kept in touch with them and you have continued the relationship, keeping your name on the tip of their tongue. They will also know how to deal with referrals, because over time you have 'trained' them, as in subtle ways you have told them the type of work you are interested in. So, not only will they give out your number, they will willingly call or email you with the prospects number. Why?

It's all because you have invested in the relationship, you have bothered to keep in touch and you have been a helpful friend. You don't sell to them all the time - you simply keep in touch in a helpful and nice manner that is meaningful to them.

Becoming a Gatekeeper!

I teach my students and members a principle called Gatekeeping. It's quite possible that you can have your customer call you when they need a plumber, plasterer, gardener, or builder for example. You become their go-to person. This might sound like a lot of work and you may even be asking why you would pass on work to other trades people, but let me tell you, firstly it is not that difficult to do when done correctly and secondly there is good reason for doing it. If you are networking (and you should be) you will have contacts in various trades, if you are joint venturing (again you should be), then you will have reciprocal arrangements with these contacts and therefore will know and trust them enough to have no problem recommending them.

The reason you want to do this is because if people are using you as a 'Gatekeeper', calling you when they need other trades and services, then when they want an electrician you will definitely be the one they call. It is amazing that many tradesmen will pay hundreds of pounds a year to belong to networking organisations and not use their membership effectively, then complain that networking doesn't work. I was a member of BNI for over nine years and I can assure you that when used correctly and strategically networking is a great tool in your marketing arsenal.

The Customer Keeper

Keeping in touch with customers is in itself an art form, you do not want to annoy them because they will hit the unsubscribe button very quickly if you keep emailing them rubbish or sending sales letters. But, if you have put the effort into building the relationship and are sending helpful information that they are interested in then they are going to be pleased to hear from you and less likely to get rid of what you send them.

We have a vast number of ways to communicate with our customers, remember the key here is to communicate, not to sell. Your objective is to keep your name on the tip of their tongue and you do this by getting in their letterbox, in their inbox, on their texts and on their phone - all so that you are the one they think of when they or someone they know wants an electrician (or any other trade).

Letters – You can find any number of reasons to send a past customer a letter. You can thank them for the work, remind them of your contacts in other trades, let them know that you have once again successfully passed your annual inspection, added a member to the team, added a service you previously didn't cover, or you might have an offer you can advise them about. Using 'lumpy mail' you could send a gift, a fridge magnet, a pen, your annual calendar or diary for example. The only limit is your imagination.

Telephone – We're happy to use the telephone up to the point of getting the job and we will organise quotes over the phone, take deposits and arrange a date for the job to be completed, yet once the job is done we rarely call to follow up. It would be so easy to call and ask something like "Did we meet your requirements? Is everything okay? Can I submit your job for my annual inspection? Did I mention while I was with you that I have a list of local trusted tradesmen I would be happy to introduce you to?" Again, no selling. Do not try to sell them anything. You are just trying to make sure they remember your name. So when their neighbour needs an electrician, you're the only one they call. When the daughter needs work done – yours is the name they remember and so you are the one they call. You see how powerful this can be?

Newsletters – It can be very difficult to get people these days to sign up to receive an online newsletter; if you have ever tried you will know what I mean. Several years ago I decided to sign up my customers by simply adding them to my newsletter responder and gave them the option to opt-out. No one ever complained about receiving the e-newsletter and very few actually opted out. I used to send out an e-newsletter once a month (via AWeber) to my list of customers, but at the time I realised many of my customers were elderly and didn't use email and were missing out, so I made it into a separate paper based newsletter. You can do either or both depending on your specific client base. I try to do newsletters as cost effectively and cheaply as possible, as I do with everything, but I also make them as effective as possible.

A typical newsletter might contain some or all of the following:

- An Article or two about some work you have recently undertaken

- A Helpful Hint, or 'Trade Secret'

- 'Sparky Chat' – the lingo of electricians e.g. what an RCD is

- A Photo of an awful job or fault you have come across

- A Quiz, with a simple prize - (bottle of wine)

- Some Personal info – e.g. been away on holiday, went to see a movie, family day out etc – make it into a story

- A Letter from a happy customer

- Congratulations to a previous competition winner with a photo

You are not looking to write a masterpiece or set up a publishing empire so keep it simple and authentic. Remember the real function here is in getting and keeping your name in their minds.

Email – This is one of my favourite methods for keeping in touch. The success of this as a marketing technique depends on two main things; first your ability to consistently collect customer and potential customer email addresses and secondly being able to send emails that are of interest and engaging for the people you send them to. I go into great detail on both of these topics inside the ToolBox member site – it would be impossible to go into great detail in a book such as this but you can download my videos on Email marketing at **www.jdewane.com/gifts**

Greetings Cards – Another excellent way to keep in touch. Not just Christmas (in fact Christmas is probably the worst time in the UK because everyone sends out Christmas cards, so it's likely your card will get lost amongst all the others). There is an endless list of other reasons for sending greeting cards though, including St Patricks Day, St Georges Day, Valentine's Day, Birthdays and Wedding Anniversaries if you know them.

Wouldn't they think it strange?!

It doesn't matter whether they think it strange, bizarre or normal, because, most importantly, it is another contact from you - so they see your name again. Greeting cards are regarded as personal and in most cases are only sent by friends and family, so by doing this you will be considered 'a friend'.

Text Messages – Can be used in a very similar way to email, sending useful information and tips from time to time.

Hopefully the above will give you some food for thought. I know it sounds time consuming to set up systems and find content for all of these communications and that is why no one really bothers to try and do it, plus it can be extremely difficult if it's done badly. However, when you know how to do it well, timing your communications properly and sending the right kind of information you will achieve easy sales without even trying to sell.

---

*"Communication and trust are two main ingredients for relationships..." – **Unknown***

ToolBox tales...

I'd been looking for some help and advice when getting my business off the ground/moving forward. My initial contact with James was via Facebook.

The initial basic advice made a lot of sense to me and I really wanted to learn more. The resources that were on offer seemed a good fit for me and where I intended to take my business, so I joined.

ToolBox tales (cont)...

The resources are useful and a constant reminder of the things that you need to be doing in order to keep the flow of enquiries/work coming in. In the early days I had to learn to trust the advice and go with it. Quickly getting over my own beliefs about certain types of marketing was key to being able to build on the early successes.

I doubt I would have made the business profitable so quickly without the help of James and My Electricians ToolBox - therefore it is definitely good value for money.

You would benefit from James' training and coaching if you are an owner of young electrical businesses who strive to be more than a 'one man band' and are serious about owning a BUSINESS, rather than a JOB. Owners who would like to be able to select which work they do rather than accepting every enquiry regardless of work type. Businesses who are just treading water but would like to be moving forwards.

I would recommend My Electricians ToolBox to any business owner who finds themselves in the situations described above.

Carl Firmstone
Stator Electrical Solutions Ltd
www.stator-electricians.co.uk

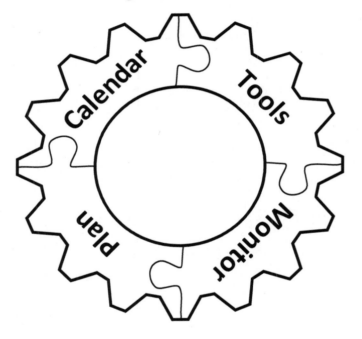

Systemise

- Calendar
- Tools
- Monitor
- Plan

"If you are too busy to build good systems, then you'll always be too busy…."

Brian Logue

Chapter 9

The Marketing **S**ystem Creator

IT IS ALL very well having the tools and knowing what to do about your marketing, however if you just have the tools and still do nothing then the results you will get will match the effort you put in. No effort equals no results. I will often get asked where I found the time to do everything and the truth is I didn't. You see, you don't have to do everything and even those things you do decide to do, much of it can be done by others or outsourced. The main thing is that you know and understand how everything works, so that you can make the right decisions for your business.

I am a great believer in systemising your marketing. There are no end of professionals who will talk to you about systemising your business as a whole but that is not what I am talking about here. I am talking about systemising your marketing, putting in place systems that ensure you are not spending all your time on your marketing or that it doesn't get forgotten due to other things (like work) getting in the way.

It's all about what you can do to ensure that you have enough work coming in to sustain you at the level you want. It's all about creating a funnel so that you can know for weeks and months in advance what work you have lined up.

I have had periods where I've known that I have three months of work in the diary. Now, in most domestic based service businesses that is unheard of. Three weeks is often as much as you could expect. More often than not many tradesmen don't have a feel for what work they have from week to week, so they go from feast to famine only thinking about their marketing when they see the diary is empty.

I believe that you should spend at least one hour a day working on your marketing. This should be purely focused on the marketing of your business and working only on those things that will either attract new customers into your business or help you maximise the results you get from your existing customers. This part of your day is not for producing certificates, writing quotes or invoices and it should be free of distractions like Facebook and email. It should be a habit you form and should be stuck to religiously. I am an early riser and for me my marketing hour was four days a week early morning often starting at 05.00 and finished for 06.00 which still gave me time to do some certs, quotes and invoices before the 'working day' started. Some of my students are happier doing their marketing hour in the evening, while others spend time over the weekend doing a block of three or four hours.

Do it in a way that suits you, but do it! Some dedicated time on your marketing is better than no time. If you do nothing, there will be no results, whereas if you do something you will get some results and the more you do the better the results you will get.

If you systemise your marketing you can control your work flow and don't have to 'panic manage' during the feast and famine phenomenon.

The Marketing System Creator

In order to systemise your marketing effectively you need to get to grips with the following: The tools you have available, a plan to use those tools, and a means of monitoring results so that you can adjust your plan.

There is a whole plethora of Marketing Tools you can use. For example...

- Leaflets
- Flyers
- Magazines / Directories
- Banner ads
- Radio
- TV
- Cinema
- Sponsorships
- Websites
- Blogs
- YouTube videos
- Facebook ads
- LinkedIn
- Twitter

And when you think outside the box there are many other creative options such as coin stickers, fridge magnets, disruption postcards and so on.

You need to work out what tools will work for you and what you are comfortable using.

It can take some people a bit of time to realise that you don't have to do everything. Think...

What am I comfortable with? - If you don't like being in front of a camera then video is not necessarily going to be your best channel.

What is getting results? No point sending out leaflets if they don't work for you.

You need to be aware of what tools you can have in your arsenal. You need to test what works and what doesn't. You need to work out what you are comfortable using and more importantly which tools best target your ideal customer.

Do not be distracted by shiny objects, don't let the salesman who calls you with 'the best deal on the planet for advertising' in his booklet distract you from what works for your business. When you understand the tools available and how you can use them you are in a much more powerful position when negotiating advertising, plus it helps with the next step - which is preparing your marketing plan.

Your Plan

Do you have a plan?

How do you know what promotions to run?

How do you know when and where you have sweet spots? And how to make the best of these?

How do you manage around periods when you are getting no work but you know the work is out there?

So, there needs to be a plan in place.

If you have figured out your niche, the type and quantity of work you want, you know what your target audience is and have identified your ideal customer, then this will all help you to formulate your plan and assist you in getting the kind of results you want.

The best and easiest way to develop a marketing plan is to follow a Marketing Calendar. If you sit down once a year and mark out key events in the year during which you want to run promotions, you can then map out in advance what tools you will use and how you will use them. Remember, it doesn't always have to be about selling - some of your promotions are simply about keeping your name and your business in your customers mind.

For example, in the lead up to Halloween 2014 I ran a three part ghost story which I sent out to my whole database during the two week build up to Halloween, but not once did I try to sell anything in the story or the emails. I got several comments long after running the story, which, I didn't even have to write by the way because I simply outlined what I wanted and outsourced it. When the story came back I simply broke it into three parts and added it to my auto-responder - the result was three engaging emails that kept my name in mind.

Another example, after the bank holiday, how many times do you get a call to say "hubby has tried to do something over the holiday, messed it up and now we need help to finish it off please!"

You can pre-empt all that because your calendar tells you! So you can send promotional emails, flyers, letters or texts such as "Are you considering any electrical work over the bank holiday. If you are then please remember you need a qualified and competent electrician for this kind of work."

A standard calendar gives us plenty of excuses to get in touch or to keep in touch, however you can also add events of your own and create marketing opportunities out of them. For example when your van is due an MOT why not use the story of having an MOT as a good way of introducing an electrical inspection or use the anniversary of your company to let people know how far you have come in the past X amount of years; again, the only limit is your imagination. The mistake that prevents most tradesmen from succeeding with this is that they firstly don't know what to say and secondly think that they have to sell in every communication.

Setting aside some time to sit with a calendar and develop your marketing plan will ensure that you are not desperately advertising when you run short of work. Instead it means that your advertising and marketing is much more effective, funnelling work into your diary. You can find a video about using a Marketing Calendar at **www.jdewane.com/gifts**

Monitoring

I cannot stress how important it is to monitor and track the results of your marketing. We discussed this briefly in the section on advertising but it is so important that it warrants mentioning again. Part of your marketing hour each day should be spent checking what is working and what is not, that way you don't waste time and money on ineffectual marketing and advertising. Tracking numbers are my favourite way to test and track advertising, however there are a number of other tools that can also help.

Tracking / unique URL's can help you to track web activity, particularly things like offers on your website or promotions that you are advertising on other online sites. Most auto-responders today come with analytics so you can work out what emails are being opened and what links in your emails are being clicked on and this can help you understand what your audience / potential customers respond to, or ignore.

You then employ a very simple feedback loop to ensure that you get the best from your promotions.

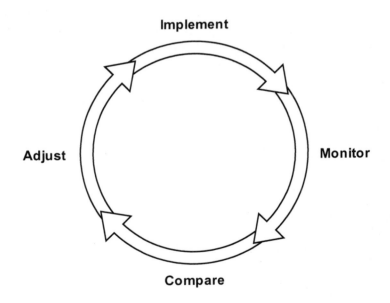

Implement

Implementation means getting your promotion or advertisement out there working for you. Often people wait until it's just perfect or they suffer from analysis paralysis where they want to know the nuts and bolts before they do anything. A great marketing idea is just that, an idea, until you put it to use. You can miss some great opportunities by waiting too long. Some people are always getting ready and never do - don't be one of those.

Monitor

By monitoring and tracking your promotions and advertisements you will know what is working and what is not. Having systems in place to track everything ensures that you are not just guessing, like Henry Ford. You don't just have a feeling for what is working and what's not, you know with 100% certainty.

Compare

By comparing the results with your control project (your best performing) you know the type of results you should be expecting. Do not necessarily compare your promotions to other tradesmen, because their business, their niche and their ideal client are not yours and vice versa.

Adjust

Only ever make small adjustments at any one time - it could be the layout, some wording, a colour or a call to action, but make your changes incrementally. Do not make huge changes in one go because if you do you will not know what elements are working and which are not.

So that, in a nut shell, is the **S.P.A.R.K.S. Blueprint™ to Marketing for Local Trades!**

If it all sounds a bit daunting just remember you do not have to do everything to make your local business a success, start small and work your way through until you find the elements that work for you. By simply reading this book you will be way ahead of your local competition and by implementing what you have learned here you will be in a position to dominate your local area for the service that you provide. Best of all **you will become the 'go-to' tradesman in your local area.**

ToolBox tales...

I first became aware of James through his presence on Twitter, which two years ago, was one of our main sources of work. Neil (my business partner) and I had just started our business and whilst we had confidence in ourselves, the quantity of work we had was very sporadic.

Out of curiosity I purchased James 'Blueprint' book, and what I read made so much sense. I decided to join 'ToolBox' as an individual, (not part of the business), because even though the cost to be a member was small, I didn't want to place a further expense on our business.

I intended being a member for a couple of months, then backing out because I had an unfounded niggling doubt about its likely effectiveness. Well, my assumption was wrong. Through what I learned from James and the Electricians ToolBox, we were able to focus on what our core business should be.

We now have constant work within a 12 mile radius of where we live, and are booked up for between 4 to 8 weeks ahead. Our turnover has increased in the last 12 months by about 30% and we are now making a real profit.

I remain a member because James inspires me when I feel lethargy setting in, (generally when things are going well). The 'ToolBox' ethos could be applied to almost any trade. James is a marketing expert, but someone who also does hands on work, so he understands the reality of his teachings.

I should add that I've never actually met James, and my account is real. If, as James repeats regularly, you put in the effort, it does work. I'd highly recommend the Electricians ToolBox

Stuart Watson
Local Leccy Ltd
www.localleccy.co.uk

Chapter 10

What Next?

YOU PICKED UP this book because you wanted the answer to finding more customers and getting more from your existing customers. I am going to guess that while reading through you've had a few 'aha' moments. Now I know this is not because I'm psychic, but, because like you, I have been there. I have had the struggles, the sleepless nights and the empty diary. I have had my moments when I wanted to throw in the towel and call it a day, but again, like you, I sought out the solution to my difficulties and acted on them.

And there is the distinction...ACTION

Do not put this book down and think to yourself *"there were some good ideas there and I will get around to doing some of it later"*. LATER WILL NEVER COME.

The businesses that succeed are the ones that use what they learn. TAKE ACTION NOW and commit to doing at least one thing today. Take out your diary and for the next three months pencil in your Marketing Hour for each day. Yes that's right make an appointment with yourself in your diary - one that cannot be broken.

You have the power to control how successful your business is!

Many people are stuck in a blame mindset where they blame their location, their lack of funds, or the competition, their customers or the government, but the bottom line is, the buck stops, and of course, starts with you. If you could add £500 - £1,000 a week to your income would it matter what the competition were doing? If you were getting the type and quantity of work that you wanted, why would you worry about what the competition were getting or what policy changes the government made? If you are focusing on what others are doing or you are looking for others to blame for your failure, your focus is not on your success.

I was once told...

"You can either make excuses or make money, but you can't do both" - **Nigel Botterill**

And it is so true, you can go online at any time into any of the trade forums and find people moaning and complaining about all sorts of reasons why they are not successful. In fact, you don't even have to go online - try the wholesaler queue, the local café or even the pub on a Friday! There are guys only too willing to line up and tell you all the hardships that stand

---

in their way and how if they could only do this or that, or if the government would only change the law, lower the tax or halt immigration etc. but...

Ask them this one question and it usually strikes them dumb...

"What did you DO today to get customers into your business?"

The reason they do not have successful businesses is not the fault of the government, the competition or the immigrants; it's because they don't have or don't know how to get and keep customers.

My invitation to you

One of the ingredients for true success is support from others. I had great support from my friends, family and a network of like-minded people I associated with. But, no one man is an island, and maybe you don't get the support from the people you think you should.

The reason for this could be that your family might want to keep you grounded and stop you from making decisions that they see as risky, or, they want to please you so they won't give their honest opinion: they simply tell you what they think you want to hear. The exact same thing can be true of friends.

My Electricians ToolBox™ members, on the other hand, all have one thing in common - the will to succeed. Each member is invested in helping his fellow members. Plus, the ToolBox holds a vast amount of resources for tradesmen to use in the marketing of their business, along with training on tried and trusted methods.

Imagine, if you were to get just one more job a month from what you learn and use in the ToolBox. With a little effort though, you will get much more than one additional job, trust me. Think about the profit for you on just one Consumer Unit or even a Rewire. I know that would easily cover your membership.

There is nothing else like the ToolBox anywhere else in the UK, nothing that's dedicated to helping tradesmen earn money from what they do. I know that you will get results fast with this system and I don't want you to miss out on this opporunity, so I have prepared a special offer only for readers of this book, I am here and ready to help and I invite you to consider becoming a member and try:

My Electricians ToolBox™for one whole month risk free

You can find all the details at **www.jdewane.com/bookoffer**

Simply subscribe as a Standard or Gold member and enjoy all the benefits for one month then, at the end of the month, if you decide it is not for you, simply cancel your membership and request a refund. You will get a full refund, no quibble.

Think about it, **how easy would it be** for you to try this for one month – **completely risk free** – and judge for yourself whether it will work for you and your business.

Of course it's not for everyone. It's not for you if…

- You don't want domestic work
- You are looking for a quick fix (this requires a little effort)
- You are a cowboy (I only want to work with people of integrity)

You see, if you don't think it is for you, if you feel it won't work for your business, then I really don't want to take money from you. I really want you to succeed, because your success is my success, so it makes sense to only have members who want to be there. Are you willing to do what it takes to succeed?

If you think **it is for you** and want to take advantage of the trial, then all you need to do is simply head over to the website at **www.jdewane.com/bookoffer** and select the level of membership you want.

When I and many others started out as self-employed electricians, there was no one or nothing to show us how to use our trade to make money. When I struggled to survive in business I could find nothing, apart from generic marketing courses or 'done for you' options. If a program like this had existed I would have jumped at the opportunity, instead I put a lot of time and effort into learning how to make marketing work for tradesmen. As time went on and I was earning more I went on courses, bought video and DVD programs, attended webinars and seminars and eventually joined mastermind groups spending in excess of £60,000 just accumulating knowledge then distilling and synthesising it so I could make it work in my business. The result of all this training and accumulation of knowledge is inside **My Electricians ToolBox™** for you to use in building your business.

I will never stop learning and growing! Today I belong to two business mastermind groups and continue to attend new marketing courses. I still buy training programs and will always be looking at new ideas, trialling and testing to figure out what works and what doesn't and even though I am now semi-retired from being on the tools I still keep my hand in; I remain a member of the IET and the NICEIC. I consult for 'local trades based businesses', developing their marketing with them, and I also regularly run live workshops about various aspects of marketing – **www.jdewane.com/live**

Whatever you decide to do going forward, I wish you every success. You have at least taken the first step towards understanding that just doing the work is not enough to be successful at your trade. You need to understand how to get and then how to keep customers. At least in reading this book I know you will never look at your business in the same way again, and that's a good thing!

I thank you for your purchase and hope that I get to meet you in person at some point either at one of the live workshops, seminars or indeed as a member of **My Electricians ToolBox™**.

But above all...

"Remember to learn and grow..."

James Dewane